Exhaustive Outline of the Entire Bible

Christopher A. Anacker

Published by: Christopher A. Anacker
                      Post Office Box 3581
                      Ventura CA 93006-3581
                      United States of America
                      www.exhaustiveoutline.com

ISBN 10: 0-9607942-3-9
ISBN 13: 978-0-9607942-3-2

ISBN 978-0-9607942-3-2

9 780960 794232 >

The Bible's Numerical Divisions

One thing you may have noticed about the numerical divisions of the
Bible's chapters and verses is that they do not always necessarily occur
at logical beginning or end points of the context, particularly the verses.
The verse numbering system found in today's Bibles do not respect the
literary structure of the content.

Frankly, the quality of the verses layout is relatively sloppy. Scholars
agree there is no consistent literary reasoning to the layout. We have
some verses that include several sentences, and some sentences that
are divided in half. Or, we have some quotations appearing in a separate
verse following a preceding verse that contains text that sets up the
quotation. Instances like these leave us to wonder why the two were
separated.

The original manuscripts of both the Old and New Testament were not
written with chapters and verses. Reportedly, it was in the year 1205 that
a Professor from Paris named Stephen Langton (who later became the
Archbishop of Canterbury) first divided the Bible into chapters and put
this into the Vulgate edition. Later, Robert Stephanus, a book printer
from Paris, further divided those chapters into verses in 1551. It is said
that he occupied himself with this task during a horseback trip from Paris
to Lyon. This is not a very studied and purposeful way to go about the
task, which may explain the apparent sloppiness.

This *Exhaustive Outline of the Entire Bible* can help you overcome the
divisional effect and focus on the content by its nature . . . by topic or
subject matter . . . and essentially ignore the versification patterns. This
way you can more quickly comprehend the ideas conveyed in the text.

Christopher Anacker

Table of Contents

GREAT CHAPTERS, STORIES, MIRACLES AND PARABLES

Great Chapters (GC) | Stories (GS) | Miracles (M) | Parables (P)

HISTORY/LAW

GENESIS

GC	1-3	God creates the heavens and the earth
GS	6-8	Noah survives the worldwide flood
M	19:24	Sodom, Gomorrah burn by fire and brimstone
	19:26	Lot's wife becomes a pillar of salt
	21:1-3	Isaac is miraculously born
GS	22:1-18	Abraham begins to sacrifice Isaac
	27:1-46	Jacob steals Esau's blessing
	37-49	Joseph rises to great power

EXODUS

GS	1:7-22; 2:10	The rescue of Moses
M	3:2	Burning bush does not consume
GS	7-14	Millions of Hebrew slaves go free
M	7:10-12	Aaron's rod becomes a serpent
	7:20-25	Water becomes blood
	8:5-14	Plague of frogs
	8:16-18	Plague of gnats
	8:20-24	Plague of flies
	9:3-6	Herds and flocks die
	9:8-11	Boils and sores
	9:22-26	Thunder and hail
	10:12-19	Plague of locusts
	10:21-23	Dark day
	12:29-30	Slaughter of firstborn
	14:21-31	Red Sea parts
	15:23-25	Waters of Marah become sweet
	16:14-35	Manna from heaven
	17:5-7	Water from the rock
GC	20	Ten Commandments

LEVITICUS

M   10:1-2   Fire consumes Nadab and Abihu

NUMBERS

M   11:1-3   Camp at Taberah burns
     16:31-35   Ground swallows Korah, Dathan, and Abiram
     17:8   Aaron's rod sprouts buds
     20:7-11   Water from the rock
     21:8-9   Bronze serpent heals

DEUTERONOMY

GC   32-34   Moses' farewell talk

<u>HISTORY/EARLY PROPHETS</u>

JOSHUA

GC   1   Challenge for Joshua
      3:14-17   River Jordan suddenly stops flowing
GS   5:10-6:26   Jericho falls; a spy story
M   6:6-25   Walls fall from shouts and trumpets
      10:12-14   Sun and moon stand still

JUDGES

GS   4   Deborah to the rescue
      6-7   Trumpets and lanterns for weapons
P   9:7-15   Trees choose a king
GS   14-17   Samson's fame and fall
M   14:1-
      16:30   Samson's strength
P   14:14   Samson's riddle
M   15:9   Water from a hollow place

RUTH

GS   1-4   A tender story of love

1 SAMUEL

GS   3   Mysterious voice in the night
M   5:1-12   Dagon falls twice; Affliction of tumors
      6:19   Slaughter of men who look into Ark
      7:10-12   Thunderstorm panics the warriors
      12:17-18   Thunder and rain in harvest

GS	16:1-13	God chooses the youngest to be king
	17	David slays the giant Goliath
	20	David and Jonathan: story of loyalty
	23-24	David and Saul: tension in a cave

2 SAMUEL

M	5:23-25	Sound of marching in balsam trees
	6:7	Slaughter of men who touch the Ark
GS	11-12	David and Bathsheba
P	12:1-4	Poor man's ewe lamb
	14:6-11	Two sons and avengers
GS	15-18	Treachery and tragedy break a father's heart

1 KINGS

GS	10	Queen of Sheba visits
M	13:4-5	Man's hand withers; altar destructs
	17:1-19:8	Drought, fire from heaven, and rain at Elijah's request; Ravens feed Elijah
	17:14-16	Oil and meal increases
	17:17-24	Widow's son rises from dead
GS	18	God outperforms the false prophets
M	20:30	Wall falls on thousands of Syrians
P	20: 35-40	Captive who escapes
	22:19-23	Micaiah's vision

2 KINGS

M	1:10-12	Captains and companies burn
	2:8	Elijah divides the River Jordan
	2:11	Whirlwind lifts Elijah to the sky
	2:14	Elisha divides the River Jordan
	2:21-22	Jericho waters become wholesome
	2:24	Bears destroy mocking boys
	3:16-20	Allies receive water
	4:2-7	Widow's oil increases
	4:32-37	Shunamrnites' son rises from the dead
	4:38-41	Deadly pottage becomes good
	4:42-44	Feeding one hundred men
	5:10-14, 27	Elisha heals leper; Gehazi becomes leprous
	6:5-7	Iron axe floats on water
	6:18-20	Soldiers go blind

	13:21	Bones revive a dead man
P	14:9	Thistle and cedar
M	19:35	Destruction of an army
	20:9-11	Sundial shadow reverses
GS	22	Josiah discovers something great

HISTORY/THE WRITINGS

1 CHRONICLES
| GC | 29:10-19 | David's great prayer |

2 CHRONICLES
| P | 25:18 | Thistle and cedar |
| M | 26:16-21 | Uzziah becomes leprous |

NEHEMIAH
| GS | 1-13 | Rebuilding of Jerusalem |

ESTHER
| GS | 1-10 | Courage and devotion |

POETRY/THE WRITINGS

JOB
GS	1-3	Job's problems
GC	36:24-	Works of God: wonders of nature
	41:34	

PSALMS
GC	19	Psalm of nature
	23	Shepherd psalm
	l00	Psalm of praise
	107	Psalm of salvation
	119	Psalm of God's word

PROVERBS
| GC | 3 | Good advice for young men and women |
| | 31:10-31 | A good wife |

MAJOR AND MINOR PROPHETS

ISAIAH

P	5:1-7	Unfruitful vineyard
	28:23-29	Plowman
GC	53	Suffering servant; Prophecy of Messiah

EZEKIEL

GC	1	Wind, fire, and strange winged creatures
P	17:2-10	Eagles and the vine
	19:2-9	Lion's whelps
	23:1-49	Two harlots
	24:3-5	Boiling pot
	31:3-18	Cedar of Lebanon
	32:1-16	Dragon in the seas
	34:1-31	Shepherds and the flock
	37:1-28	Dry bones in the valley
	47:1-23	Living waters

DANIEL

M	3:19-27	Deliverance from a fiery furnace
	6:16-23	Deliverance from the lions

AMOS

P	7:1-3	Vision of locusts
	7:4-6	Fire devouring the deep
	7:7-9	Plumb line
	8:1-3	Basket of summer fruit

JONAH

M	2:1-10	Deliverance from the great whale

ZECHARIAH

P	1:7-17	Four horsemen who patrol the earth
	1:18-21	Four horns and four smiths
	2:1-13	Man with measuring line
	4:1-14	Lampstand and two olive trees
	5:1-4	Flying scroll
	5:5-11	Ephah of iniquity contains a woman
	6:1-8	Four chariots
	11:3-17	Shepherd with staffs Union and Grace

The Gospels

MATTHEW

GS	2:13-18	Christ child flees murder
	4:1-11	Jesus rejects Satan
P	5:14-16	Lamp under a bushel
	7:3-5	Speck and log
	7:24-27	House on rock, house on sand
M	8:2-3	Leprosy leaves a man
	8:5-13	Paralysis leaves the servant
	8:14-15	Fever leaves a woman
	8:23-26	Jesus stills a storm
	8:28-32	Jesus casts out demons
	9:2-7	Paralysis leaves a man
P	9:15	Wedding guests
	9:16-17	New wine in old wineskins
M	9:18-26	Daughter rises back to life
	9:20-22	Woman stops bleeding
	9:27-31	Two men receive their sight
	9:32-33	Man receives his speech
P	11:16-17	Children at play
M	12:10-13	Man's hand becomes whole
	12:22	Man receives his sight and speech
P	12:43-45	Seven unclean spirits
	13:18-30	Sower
	13:31-32	Mustard seed
	13:33	Leaven
	13:44	Hidden treasure
	13:45-46	Pearl of great price
	13:47-48	Full net
	13:52	Old and new treasures
M	14:15-21	Five thousand receive food
	14:25-27	Jesus walks on the sea
	15:21-28	Demon leaves daughter
	15:32-38	Four thousand receive food
	17:1-13	Transfiguration
	17:14-18	Epilepsy leaves the boy
	17:24-27	Coin in the fish mouth Parables
	18:12-14	Sheep once lost, now found
	18:23-34	Unmerciful servant
	20:1-16	Laborers in the vineyard

	20:30-34	Man receives his sight
	21:19	Fig tree withers
P	21:28-32	Father and two sons
	21:33-41	Vineyard and husbandmen
	21:42-45	Rejected stones
	22:1-14	Marriage of the king's son
	24:32	Young leaves of the fig tree
	25:1-13	Wise and foolish maidens
	25:14-30	Talents
	25:31-46	Sheep and goats
GS	26:1-28:20	Denial, murder, and resurrection of Christ

MARK

	1:23-26	Demon leaves a man
M	1:23-26	Demon leaves a man
	1:30-31	Fever leaves a woman
	1:40-41	Leprosy leaves a man
	2:3-12	Paralysis leaves a man
P	2:19-22	New wine in old wineskins
M	3:1-5	Man's hand becomes whole
P	4:3-9	Sower
	4:21-23	Lamp under a bushel
	4:26-29	Growth of a seed of grain
	4:31-32	Mustard seed
M	4:35-39	Jesus stills a storm
	5:1-13	Jesus casts out demons
	5:22-42	Daughter rises back to life
	5:25-29	Woman stops bleeding
	6:35-44	Five thousand receive food
	6:48-51	Jesus walks on the sea
	7:24-30	Demon leaves daughter
	7:31-37	Man receives his hearing and speech
	8:1-9	Four thousand receive food
	8:22-26	Man receives his sight
	9:1-13	Transfiguration
	9:17-27	Epilepsy leaves the boy
	10:46-52	Man receives his sight
	11:14	Fig tree withers
P	12:1-8	Vineyard and husbandmen
	12:10-11	Rejected stones
	12:19-20	Wedding guests
	13:34-36	Watchful doorkeeper

| | 13:38 | Young leaves of the fig tree |
| GS | 14:1-16:20 | Murder, resurrection, and ascension of Christ |

LUKE

	4:1-13	Jesus rejects Satan
GS		
M	4:28-30	Jesus passes unseen through crowds
	4:33-35	Demon leaves a man
	4:38-39	Fever leaves a woman
	5:1-11	Great catch of fish
	5:12-13	Leprosy leaves a man
	5:18-25	Paralysis leaves the man
P	5:34-35	Wedding guests
	5:36-39	New wine in old wineskins
M	6:6-11	Man's hand becomes whole
P	6:41-42	Speck and log
	6:48-49	House on rock, house on sand
M	7:1-10	Paralysis leaves the servant
	7:11-15	Widow's son rises back to life
P	7:31-32	Children at play
	7:41-50	Two debtors
	8:5-8	Sower
	8:16-18	Lamp under a bushel
M	8:22-24	Jesus stills a storm
	8:26-33	Jesus casts out demons
	8:41-56	Daughter rises back to life
	8:43-48	Woman stops bleeding
	9:10-17	Five thousand receive food
	9:28-36	Transfiguration
	9:37-42	Epilepsy leaves the boy
P	10:30-37	Good Samaritan
	11:5-8	Friend at midnight
M	11:14	Man receives his sight and speech
P	11:24-26	Seven unclean spirits
	12:16-21	Rich fool
	12:35-40	Waiting servants
	12:42-48	Faithful and wise servant
	13:6-9	Barren fig tree
M	13:11-13	Woman stands up straight
P	13:18-19	Mustard seed
	13:20-21	Leaven
	13:25-27	Shut door

M	14:1-4	Dropsy leaves the man
P	14:7-11	Places of honor
	14:16-24	Great banquet
	14:28-33	Tower; the warring king
	15:4-7	Sheep once lost, now found
	15:8-10	Coin once lost, now found
	15:11-32	Prodigal son
	16:1-8	Dishonest steward
	16:19-31	Rich man and Lazarus
	17:7-10	Farmer and his servant
M	17:11-19	Leprosy leaves ten men
P	18:1-8	Unrighteous judge
	18:9-14	Pharisee and tax collector
M	18:35-43	Man receives his sight
P	19:12-27	Nobleman and the ten pounds
	20:9-16	Vineyard and husbandmen
	20:17-18	Rejected stones
	21:29-30	Young leaves of the fig tree
Gs	22:1-24:53	Murder, resurrection, ascension of Christ
M	22:50-51	Servant receives back his ear

JOHN

M	2:1-11	Water becomes wine
	4:46-54	Fever leaves the official's son
	5:1-9	Invalidity leaves the man
	6:1-14	Five thousand receive food
	6:19-20	Jesus walks on the sea
P	6:25-29	Bread of life
M	8: 59	Jesus passes through the crowd
	9:1-7	Man receives his sight
P	10:1-39	Shepherd and the sheep
M	11:38-44	Lazarus rises back to life
GS	11:45-21:25	Denial, murder, and resurrection of Christ
P	15:1-27	Vine and the branches
M	18:5-6	Soldiers fall to the ground
	21:1-14	Catch of 153 fish

ACTS

M	1:9-11	Ascension of Christ
	2:1-47	Tongues of fire
	2:4-11	Gift of tongues

	3:1-26	Lameness leaves a man
	5:1-11	Ananias and Sapphira die
	5:12-16	Sickness leaves a man
	5:17-21	Angel opens prison doors
	7:55-56	Stephen sees Christ at Father's right side
GS	8	African converts to the Way
M	8: 6-7	Philip casts out demons
GS	9	Saul becomes a Christian
M	9:1-9	Christ appears to Saul
	9:17-19	Ananias restores Saul's sight
	9:33-34	Paralysis leaves a man
	9:36-41	Peter revives Tabitha to life
	10:3-6;	Vision of Cornelius
	30-32	
P	10:9-11:10	Vision of clean and unclean animals
M	10:44-48	Gift of tongues
	11:27-28	Prophecies of Agabus
	12:6-10	Peter's release from prison
	13:9-11	Peter blinds Elymus
	14:8-10	Man walks for first time
GS	16	Philippian jailer converts to the Way
M	16:9	Paul's vision of the Macedonian man
	16:16-18	Paul casts out the divining spirit
	16:25-26	Earthquake at Philippi
	19:11-12	Diseases leave many
	19:13-16	Demons chase Jewish exorcists
	20:9-12	Paul raises Entychus to life
	21:10-11	Prophecies of Agabus
	22:6-11	Christ appears to Paul
	22:12-13	Ananias restores Paul's sight
	22:17-21	Christ appears to Paul
	23:11	Christ appears to Paul
	26:12-18	Christ appears to Paul
GS	27-28	Paul's shipwreck
M	27:23-24	Christ appears to Paul
	28:3-6	Viper bite does not harm Paul
	28:8-9	Diseases leave many

EPISTLES OF PAUL

1 CORINTHIANS
GS   13   Love

PHILIPPIANS
GS   4   Secret of happiness

GENERAL EPISTLES

HEBREWS
GS   11   Great heroes of faith

APOCALYPSE

REVELATION
M   1:10-11   Visions of John
     4:1-22:21   Visions of John
GS   21-22   City of God — a new world is corning

Notes:_____

_____

_____

_____

_____

_____

_____

_____

_____

_____

_____

_____

_____

_____

_____

_____

_____

_____
_____
_____
_____
_____
_____
_____
_____
_____
_____
_____
_____
_____
_____
_____
_____
_____
_____
_____
_____
_____
_____
_____
_____
_____
_____
_____
_____
_____
_____
_____
_____
_____
_____
_____
_____
_____
_____
_____
_____
_____

GENESIS		**History/Law**
1:1		God creates the heavens and the earth
	2	Earth becomes void
	3-5	First day: light and dark
	6-8	Second day: sky
	9-13	Third day: dry land, plants, and trees
	14-19	Fourth day: sun, moon, and stars
	20-23	Fifth day: birds, fish, and reptiles
	24-31	Sixth day: animals and Adam
2:1-3		Seventh day: the Sabbath
	4-14	God places Adam in the Garden of Eden
	15-17	Forbidden tree
	18-24	God creates Eve
3:1-13		Even, then Adam, disobeys God
	14-15	God sets a curse on the serpent
	16-19	God sets a curse on the Adam and Eve
	20-24	God sends Adam & Eve from Garden of Eden
4:1-7		Cain and Abel sacrifice to God
	8-16	Cain kills Abel
	17-24	Cain's children
	25-26	Eve bears Seth
5:1-24		Adam's descendants
	25-32	Methuselah and Noah
6:1-4		Days of the mighty men
	5-8	God to drown all evil men
	9-22	God commands Noah to build the ark
7:1-10		God's command to fill the ark
	11-16	God sends the flood
	17-24	Waters cover all mountains
8:1-5		Waters subside
	6-12	Noah sends a raven and a dove
	13-19	Noah returns to dry land
	20-22	Noah builds an altar of sacrifice
9:1-7		God blesses Noah
	8-19	God's covenant with Noah
	20-28	Noah curses Canaan; blesses Shem
I0:1-20		Descendants of Noah's sons
	21-32	Shem's sons
11:1-9		Tower of Babel
	10-26	Shem's descendants
	27-32	Abram's genealogy

12:1-9		God calls Abram out of Haran
13:1		Abram goes to Egypt
	2-7	Abram and Lot separate
	3-18	Lot chooses Sodom
14:1-12		Kings' soldiers do battle
	13-16	Abram delivers Lot
	17-24	Melchizedek blesses Abram
15:1-16		God's covenant with Abram
	17-21	God promises a land
16:1-6		Hagar bears a child of Abram's
	7-16	God calls the child Ishmael
17:1-14		God's covenant of circumcision
	15-27	God's promise to Sarai
18:1-15		Lord and two angels visit Abram
	16-21	God to destroy Sodom and Gomorrah
	22-33	Abraham pleads for Sodom
19:1-14		Two angels visit Lot again
	15-23	Lot and his family flee Sodom
	24-29	God destroys Sodom and Gomorrah
	30-38	Sin of Lot's daughters
20:1-7		Abimelech takes Abraham's wife
	8-18	Abimelech apologizes to Abraham
21:1-7		Sarah bears Isaac
	8-14	Abraham casts out Hagar and Ishmael
	15-21	Hagar and Ishmael live in wilderness of Paran
	22-34	Abraham and Abimelech make a covenant
22:1-8		God tests Abraham
	9-24	Abraham begins to sacrifice his son Isaac
23:1-29		Sarah dies and Abraham buries her
24:1-14		Abraham's servant searches for wife for Isaac
	15-33	Rebekah at the well
	34-49	Servant describes his errand
	50-61	Rebekah goes with the servant
	62-67	Isaac and Rebekah marry
25:1-6		Abraham takes another wife, Keturah
	7-11	Abraham dies
	12-18	Ishmael's descendants
	19-26	Isaac's descendants
	27-34	Esau sells his birthright
26:1-16		Isaac dwells in Gerar
	17-33	Isaac quarrels with the herdsmen

	34-35	Esau marries Judith and Basemath
27:1-4		Isaac prepares to bless Esau
	5-17	Rebekah schemes with Jacob
	18-29	Jacob steals Esau's blessing
	30-40	Esau learns of the trick
	41-46	Rebekah's scheme
28:1-9		Isaac sends Jacob to Laban
	10-22	Jacob's dream at Bethel
29:1-8		Jacob's trip
	9-14	Jacob meets Rachel
	15-30	Jacob marries Leah and Rachel
	31-35	Jacob's children
30:1-24		Sons of Bilhah and Zilpah
	25-43	Jacob bargains with Laban
31:1-16		Jacob plans to return home
	17-32	Jacob flees from Laban
	33-42	Rachel steals the household gods
	43-55	Jacob and Laban make a covenant
32:1-12		Jacob prepares to meet Esau
	13-21	Jacob's present for Esau
	22-32	Jacob wrestles with the Lord
33:1-14		Jacob and Esau meet
	15-20	Jacob journeys to Shechem
34:1-17		Hamar defiles Dinah
	18-31	Simeon and Levi revenge Dinah
35:1-15		God renews the covenant with Jacob
	16-26	Rachel bears Benjamin; Rachel dies
	27-29	Isaac dies
36:1-19		Esau's descendants
	20-30	Seir's sons
	31-43	Kings of Edom
37:1-11		Joseph's dream; his brothers hate him
	12-24	Joseph's brothers plot to kill him
	25-36	Joseph's brothers sell him to traders
38:1-11		Judah marries Shua's daughter
	12-23	Judah sins with Tamar
	24-30	Tamar bears Perez and Zerah
39:1-18		Joseph prospers, keeps God's pure values
	19-23	Joseph's master casts him into prison unjustly
40:1-8		Joseph says God interprets dreams
	9-15	Butler's dream

	16-23	Baker's dream
41:1-13		Pharaoh's dream
	14-24	Pharaoh tells his dream to Joseph
	25-36	Joseph tells Pharaoh its meaning
	37-45	Pharaoh makes Joseph a ruler
	46-57	Dream comes true
42:1-5		Joseph's brothers visit Egypt
	6-28	Joseph meets his brothers
	29-38	Ten sons report to Jacob
43:1-15		Second trip to Egypt
	16-25	Joseph's brothers return to Egypt
	26-34	Joseph eats with his brothers
44:1-13		Missing silver cup
	14-17	Joseph's brothers bow before him
	18-34	Judah pleads for Benjamin
45:1-15		Joseph reveals his identity
	16-28	Pharaoh invites Joseph's kin to Egypt
46:1-7		Jacob goes to Egypt
	8-27	Jacob's descendants
	28-34;	Joseph settles father and brothers in Egypt
47:1-12		
	13-26	Land policies of Joseph
	27-31	Joseph's promise to Jacob
48:1-22		Jacob blesses Joseph's sons
49:1-27		Jacob blesses his sons
	28;	Jacob dies
	50:1-3	
50:4-14		Joseph and brothers bury Jacob in Canaan
	15-21	Joseph forgives his brother's sin against him

EXODUS — History/Law

1:1-14		New king of Egypt oppresses the Israelites
	15-22	Pharaoh's command to the midwives
2:1-10		Daughter of Levi bears Moses
	11-25	Moses commits a crime then flees to Midian
3:1-6		God speaks to Moses from a burning bush
	7-12	God commissions Moses
	13-22	God's name is I AM WHO I AM
4:1-17		God equips Moses
	18-31	Moses starts for Egypt
5:1-9		Pharaoh refuses to let the Israelites go

	10-21	Taskmasters increase the Israelites' work
	22-23;	God promises to deliver the Israelites
	6:1-13	
6:14-27		Israel's genealogy
	28-30;	Aaron to speak for Moses
	7:1-7	
7:8-13		Rod becomes a serpent
	14-24	Water becomes blood
	25;	Plague of frogs
	8:1-15	
8:16-19		Plague of gnats
	20-32	Swarms of flies
9:1-7		Egyptian cattle die
	8-12	Plague of boils and sores
	13-21	God threatens more plagues
	22-35	Plague of hail and fire
10:1-11		Moses and Aaron ask for release
	12-20	Plague of locusts
	21-29	Plague of darkness
11:1-10		God announces the last plague
12:1-13		God institutes the Passover
	14-20	Observing the Passover Week
	21-28	Killing the Passover lamb
	29-36	God kills all the firstborn Egyptian children
	37-42	Israelites begin leaving
	43-51	Law of the Passover
13:1-2		God's command to consecrate the firstborn
	3-10	Feast of Unleavened Bread
	11-16	God's command to set apart the firstborn
	17-22	God leads in a pillar of cloud and fire
14:1-4		God orders to camp in front of Pi-ha-hiroth
	5-20	Pharaoh sends his soldiers after the Israelites
	21-30	Israelites cross the Red Sea
15:1-18		Song of Moses
	1-21	Song of Miriam
	22-27	Israelites in the wilderness of Shur
16:1-12		Israelites in the wilderness of Sin
	13-21	God gives quails and manna
	22-36	God gives food for the Sabbath
17:1-7		God gives water from the rock
	8-16	Israelites defeat the Amaleks

18:1-12		Jethro comes to Moses
	13-27	Jethro tells Moses to select judges
19:1-9		Israelites in the wilderness of Sinai
	10-15	God tells Moses to consecrate His people
	16-25	Moses meets God on Mount Sinai
20:1-20		Ten Commandments
	21-26	God tells Moses to make an altar of earth
21:1-11		Slaves
	12-17	Murderers
	18-27	Quarreling and fighting
	28-36;	Livestock
	22:1,4	
22:2-5		Property
	16-31;	Personal actions
	23:1-9	
23:10-13		Sabbath
	14-19	Appointed Feasts
	20-33	God promises to protect His people
24:1-11		Israelites accept the covenant with God
	12-18	Moses on mountain forty days and nights
25:1-9		Moses to receive articles for the tabernacle
	10-22	Ark of God
	23-30	Table
	31-40	Lampstand
26:l-6		Tabernacle
	7-30	Tabernacle decor
	31-37	Veil
27:1-8		Altar
	9-19	Court of the tabernacle
	20-21	Oil for the lamp
28:1-14		Garments for the priests
	15-30	Priest's breastpiece
	31-43	Priest's robe
29:1-9		Consecrating the priests
	10-14	Offering for sin
	15-18	Offering by fire
	19-37	Things to sacrifice when consecrating priests
	38-46	Altar of offering by fire
30:1-10		Altar of incense
	11-16	Offering the halfshekels
	17-38	Laver, oil and incense

18

31:1-11		Workmen
	12-18	God's command to keep the Sabbath
32:1-10		Aaron makes a golden calf
	11-14	Moses pleads with God
	15-24	Moses destroys the golden calf
	25-35	Sons of Levi slaughter persons not for God
33:1-16		God renews the covenant
	17-23	Moses beholds God's glory
34:1-10		Second tables of stone
	11-17	God warns against heathen idols
	18-28	Appointed Feasts
	29-35	Moses' face shines
35:1-19		Moses tells the Israelites: build the tabernacle
	20-29	Things people offer for the tabernacle
	30-35; 36:1-7	Moses gathers the workmen
36:8-19		Curtains and the cover for the tent
	20-34	Frames
	35-38	Veil
37:1-9		Bezalel constructs the ark
	10-24	Table and the lampstand
	25-29	Altar for incense
38:1-8		Altar for offering fire
	9-23	Court of the tabernacle
	24-31	Valuable metals
39:1-7		Garments for the priests
	8-21	Priest's breastplate
	22-31	Robe of the ephod
	32-43	Moses blesses the finished work
40:1-15		Moses learns how to assemble the tabernacle
	16-33	How Moses obeys
	34-38	God's glory fills the tabernacle
LEVITICUS		**History/Law**
1:1-17		Offering by fire from the herds, flocks, birds
2:1-10		Offering cereal by fire
	11-16	Leaven and salt
3:1-17		Offering for peace
4:1-12		Offering for sins of the priest
	13-21	Offering for sins of the people
	22-26	Offering for sins of a ruler

	27-35	Offering for sins of common people
5:1-6		Acts requiring an offering for sin
	7-13	Offering for sins of the poor
	14-19;	Offering for guilt
	6:1-7	
6:8-13		Offering by fire
	14-23	Offering cereal
	24-30	Offering for sin
7:1-10		Offering for guilt
	11-21	Offering for peace
	22-27	Forbidden portions
	28-38	Portion for priests
8:1-13		Moses anoints the priests
	14-21	Moses offers for the sin of the priests
	22-29	Moses offers for ordaining the priests
	30-36	Seven days to anoint the priests
9:1-14		Eighth day, Moses offers for sin of the priests
	15-24	Moses offers for the people
10:1-7		Nadab and Abihu die for offering unholy fire
	3-11	God commands Aaron on the priests
	12-20	Eating holy food
11:1-23		Clean animals
	24-47	Unclean animals
12:1-8		Purifying a woman
13:1-8		Skin diseases
	9-46	Leprosy and tests for leprosy
	47-59	Leprosy in garments
14:1-32		Cleansing of lepers
	33-57	Leprosy in houses
15:1-18		Uncleanness in men
	19-33	Uncleanness in women
16:1-10		Ceremony of atonement
	11-19	Offering for sin of the priests and the people
	20-28	Goat sent into the wilderness
	29-34	The Day of Atonement
17:1-9		Special creatures for sacrifice
	10-16	Animal blood; creatures torn by beasts
18:1-23		Unlawful sexual relationships and acts
	24-30	Warning about defiling oneself
19:1-37		Various statutes: harvesting, servant's wages
20:1-21		Punishing for various sins

	22-27	God's command to be holy
21:1-15		Sanctifying the priests
	16-24	Priests with deformities
22:1-16		Priests and the holy things
	17-33	Offering unblemished animals
23:1-3		Laws of the Sabbath
	4-5	Passover
	6-8	Feast of Unleavened Bread
	9-14	Ceremony of the wavesheaf
	15-22	Pentecost
	23-25	Feast of Trumpets
	26-32	Day of Atonement
	33-35; 37-44	Feast of Tabernacles
	36	Last Great Day
24:1-9		The oil and the shewbread
	10-16	Blasphemers of the Lord's name to die
	17-23	Eye for eye, tooth for tooth
25:1-24		Sabbath and jubilee years
	25-34	Redeeming property
	35-38	Money-lending
	39-55	Redeeming servants
26:1-13		God will bless for obeying Him
	14-39	God will punish for disobeying Him
	40-46	Lord would renew the covenant
27:1-8		Vows involving persons
	9-13	Vows involving animals
	14-25	Vows involving house and land
	26-29	Devoted things
	30-34	Redeeming the tithe

NUMBERS — History/Law

1:1-16		Census of the Israelites
	17-46	Tribes and their sizes
	47-54	Levites not in count
2:1-34		Camps and tribal leaders
3:1-4		Sons of Aaron
	5-39	Numbering and duties of the Levites
	40-51	Numbering of firstborn males
4:1-20		Sons of Kohath
	21-28	Sons of Gershon

	29-33	Sons of Merari
	34-49	Results of the census
5:1-4		Lord's command concerning the unclean
	5-10	Restituting for a sin
	11-22	Law about persons suspected of adultery
	23-31	Test for persons suspected of adultery
	6:1-21	Law for a Nazirite
	22-27	Aaron to bless the Israelites
7:1-11		Dedicating the altar
	12-23	Offerings of Nahshon and Nethanel
	24-35	Offerings of Eliab and Elizur
	36-47	Offerings of Shelumiel and Eliasaph
	48-59	Offerings of Elishama and Gamaliel
	60-71	Offerings of Abidan and Ahiezer
	72-83	Offerings of Pagiel and Ahira
	84-89	Offering for the altar
	8:1-4	Lampstand
	5-13	Purifying the Levites
	14-26	Levites are for the holy services
9:1-14		Passover command
	15-23	Cloud by day, fire by night
10:1-10		Two silver trumpets
	11-32	Israelites set out from Sinai
	33-36	Ark and the cloud
11:1-3		People complain
	4-9	Looks and taste of Manna
	10-15	Moses asks for meat
	16-23	God's reply to Moses
	24-30	Seventy elders prophesy
	31-35	God sends quails for meat
12:1-8		Miriam and Aaron oppose Moses
	9-16	Miriam becomes leprous
13:1-24		Twelve spies go to Canaan
	25-33	Spies return
14:1-10		Israelites rebel
	11-19	Lord becomes angry
	20-38	Sentence of forty years in the wilderness
	39-45	Amalekites and Canaanites defeat Israelites
15:1-21		God requires offerings from the Israelites
	22-31	Offering for sins done unwittingly
	32-36	Israelites stone and kill a Sabbath breaker

	37-41	Tassels of remembrance
16:1-14		Korah rebels
	15-24	Moses prays for the people
	25-40	Ground swallows up the rebels
	41-50	Plague on the people
17:1-13		Aaron's rod sprouts forth buds
18:1-7		Duties of the Levites
	8-20	Priests' portion
	21-24	Tithe for the Levites
	25-32	Levites' tithe of the tithe
19:1-19		Purifying the unclean
	20-22	Penalty for not cleansing
20:1-13		Water from the rock
	14-21	Edomites refuse to let the Israelites pass
	22-29	Aaron dies
21:1-3		Lord gives Canaanites to Israelites
	4-9	Lord sends fiery serpents among Israelites
	10-20	Israelites march on
	21-30	Israelites capture Sihon
	31-35	Israelites capture Og
22:1-14		God forbids Balaam to go to Balak
	15-20	God lets Balaam go
	21-30	Balaam's ass speaks
	31-35	Angel warns Balaam
	36-40	Balaam visits Balak
	41;	Balaam blesses Balak's enemies
23:1-12		
23:13-24		Balaam blesses Balak's enemies again
	25;	Balaam blesses Balak's enemies again
24:1-9		
	10-14	Balak becomes angry with Balaam
	15-25	Balaam blesses Balak's enemies again
25:1-18		Israelites worship other gods
26:1-4		God asks for another census
	5-51	Numbers of the tribes
	5-11	Reuben
	12-14	Simeon
	15-18	Gad
	19-22	Judah
	23-25	Issachar
	26-27	Zebulun

	28-34	Manasseh
	35-37	Ephraim
	38-41	Benjamin
	42-43	Dan
	44-47	Asher
	48-51	Taphtali
	52-56	Dividing the land
	57-65	Number of Levites
27:1-11		Daughters of Zelophehad
	12-23	God selects Joshua to succeed Moses
28:1-8		Offering by fire daily
	9-10	Offering on the Sabbath
	11-15	Offering at the new moon
	16	Lord's Passover
	17-25	Feast of Unleavened Bread
	26-31	Offering on Feast of First Fruits
29:1-6		Offering on Feast of Trumpets
	7-11	Offering on Day of Atonement
	12-34	Offering on Feast of Tabernacles
	35-40	Last Great Day
30:1-16		Vows
31:1-12		Israelites slay Midianites
	13-24	Purifying the captors and their captives
	25-47	Dividing the booty
	48-54	Articles offered from officers and captains
32:1-15		Reuben and Gad settle in Gilead
	16-27	Others to settle west of the Jordan
	28-42	Half of the tribe of Manasseh settle in Gilead
33:1-49		Stages of trip from Egypt to Canaan
	50-56	Possessing Canaan
34:1-15		Canaan's boundaries
	16-29	God chooses men to divide the land
35:1-8		Cities for the Levites
	9-28	Cities of refuge
	29-34	Witnesses and ransom
36:1-13		Marrying heiresses

DEUTERONOMY   History/Law

1:1-8		God's command to take the Promised Land
	9-18	Appointment of leaders
	19-25	Report of the spies

	26-40	Murmur of the Israelites
	41-46	Amorites' defeat of the Israelites
2:1-25		Forty years in the wilderness
	26-37	Israelites' capture of the Sihonites
3:1-11		Israelites' capture of the Ogs
	12-22	Distribution of the land
	23-29	God forbids Moses to cross Jordan
4:1-14		Command for Israelites to obey
	15-24	Warning about graven images
	25-31	Results of worshipping idols
	32-40	Israelites are the chosen of God
	41-43	Cities of refuge
	44-49	Testimonies, statutes, and ordinances
5:1-21		Ten Commandments
	22-33	God and Moses at Mount Sinai
6:1-3		Purpose of the Law
	4-25	Teach & remember these words
7:1-5		Destroy foreigners. false religions
	6-16	Israelites are holy to God
	17-26	God will defeat the enemies
8:1-10		God is bringing Israelites into a good land
	11-20; 9:1-5	Warning to remember the Lord
9:6-12		Warning to remember the tables of stone
	13-24	Golden calf
	25-29	Praying to the Lord
10:1-11		Second tables of stone
	12-22	God requires Israelites to fear Him
11:1-7		Command to love God
	8-25	Keep the Commandments
	19-21	Teach children the Commandments
	22-32	Blessing and a curse
12:1-14		Sacrifice at the place the Lord chooses
	15-28	Offertory food Israelites may eat
	29-32	Israelites not to serve false gods
13:1-11		Command to kill false prophets and idolators
	12-18	Command to destroy idolatrous cities
14:1-2		Restrictions on cuts and baldness
	3-21	Clean and unclean animals
	22-28	Tithes
15:1-11		Sabbath year of release

	12-18	Command to free Hebrew slaves
	19-23	Offering the firstlings
16:1-8		Passover
	9-12	Feast of Weeks
	13-15	Feast of Tabernacles
	16-17	Males before God three times a year
	18-20	Appointing judges and officers
	21-22; 17:1	Blemished ox or sheep
17:2-13		Ruling
	14-20	A man becoming a king
18:1-8		Portion for the priests
	9-14	Forbidden pagan customs
	15-22	Promise of a prophet
19:1-13		Cities of refuge for murderers
	14	Landmarks
	15-21	Witnesses
20:1-9		Serving in the military
	10-20	Besieging a city
21:1-9		Sacrificing for an unknown murderer
	10-14	Captive wives
	15-21	Sons
	22-23	Sentencing a man to die
22:1-12		Statutes: brother's ox, proper garments
	13-30	Sexual relationships
23:1-8		Persons excluded from the assembly
	9-14	Keeping camp clean during war
	15-25	Human relationships
24:1-5		Divorce and marriage
	6-15	Protecting the poor
	16-22	Innocent and the needy
25:1-6		Various statutes
26:1-11		Offering the first fruits
	12-19	Third year tithe
27:1-14		Altar at Mount Ebal
	15-26	Twelve curses at Mount Ebal
28:1-14		Blessings for obeying the Lord
	15-68	Curses for disobeying the Lord
29:1-15		Command to keep this covenant
	16-29	Israelites not to forsake the covenant
30:1-10		Rewards for returning to the Lord

	11-20	Advice to love and obey the Lord
31:1-8		Moses appoints Joshua
	9-13	Command to teach the Law
	14-23	Lord tells Moses he will soon die
	24-30	Command about this book of law
32:1-14		Song of Moses: God's love for His people
	15-33	Punishment of the Israelites
	34-47	Lord kills and makes alive
	48-52	Lord summons Moses to die
33:1-29		Moses blesses the tribes of Israel
34:1-12		Moses dies

JOSHUA — **History/Early Prophets**

JOSHUA		**History/Early Prophets**
1:1-9		Lord's instructions to Joshua
	10-18	Israelites prepare to cross the Jordan
2:1-21		Two spies go to Jericho
	22-24	Spies return
3:1-6		Command to follow the Ark of the Covenant
	7-13	Lord's command to stand still in the Jordan
	14-17	Israelites cross on dry land
4:1-14		Twelve stones of memorial
	15-24; 5:1	Israelites finish crossing the Jordan
5:2-9		Joshua circumcises the Israelites
	10-12	Israelites keep Passover at Gilgal
	13-15	Joshua and the man with a sword
6:1-14		Israelites capture Jericho
	15-21	Israelites destroy all in Jericho
	22-27	Joshua saves Rahab
7:1-15		Joshua's men killed at Ai
	16-26	Israelites stone Achan
8:1-9		Plan to capture Ai
	10-23	Israelites capture Ai
	24-29	Israelites slaughter the people of Ai
	30-35	Joshua erects an altar in Mount Ebal
9:1-15		Gibeonites lie
	16-26	Gibeonites become slaves
10:1-11		Israelites slaughter warriors of the Amorites
	12-14	God makes the sun stand still
	15-43	Israelites capture all of the South
11:1-5		Kings of the north ally against the Israelites

	6-15	Soldiers battle by the waters of Merom
	16-23	Israelites capture all the North
12:1-6		Israelites capture the East of Jordan
	7-24	Israelites capture the West of Jordan
13:1-7		Land yet to be captured
	8-14	Land east of the Jordan
	15-23	Land of the Reubenites
	24-28	Land of the Gadites
	29-31	Land of the Manassites
	32-33;	Cities, pastures, cattle for the Levites
	14:1-5	
14:6-15		Caleb receives Hebron
15:1-12		Boundaries of Judah
	13-19	Caleb's portion
	20-63	Cities of Judah
16:	1-4	Land of Joseph
	5-10	Land of the Ephraimites
17:1-13		Manasseh's portion
	14-18	Joseph's tribe needs more land
18:1-10		Men survey the land; Joshua casts lots
	11-28	Land of Benjamin
19:1-11		Land of Simeon
	10-16	Land of Zebulun
	17-23	Land of Issachar
	24-31	Land of Asher
	32-39	Land of Naphtali
	40-51	Land of Dan
20:1-9		Six cities of refuge
21:1-42		Cities for the Levites
	43-45	God fulfills His promise
22:1-6		Joshua blesses three tribes
	7-12	Altar by the Jordan
	13-20	Israelites accuse three tribes of wrongdoing
	21-29	Reason for building the altar
	30-34	Israelites approve the reason
23:1-16		Joshua speaks to the top people
24:1-15		Joshua's last message
	16-28	Israelites chose to serve the Lord
	29-33	Joshua dies

JUDGES		**History/Early Prophets**
1:1-21		Judeans and Simeonites conquer Canaanites
	22-36	Foreigners live with the tribes
2:1-5		Israelites break the covenant
	6-10	Joshua dies
	11-15	Israelites serve the Baals
	16-23	Lord raises up judges
3:1-6		Lord leaves foreigners to test the Israelites
	7-11	Othniel delivers Israelites from Cushan-rish
	12-31	Ehud delivers the Israelites from the Moabites
4:1-10		Deborah judges Israel
	11-16	Barak kills Sisera's soldiers
	17-23	Jael kills Sisera
5:1-31		Song of Deborah
6:1-6		Midianites raid the Israelites
	7-10	Prophet speaks
	11-18	Lord commands Gideon to kill Midianites
	19-24	Angel burns Gideon's meat, cakes
	25-35	Gideon destroys the altar of Baal
	36-40	Gideon puts out fleece for a sign from God
7:1-8		Gideon chooses three hundred men
	9-18	Gideon and Purah spy the Midianites at camp
	19-25	Gideon and his men defeat the Midianites
8:1-3		Men of Ephraim upbraid Gideon
	4-9	Officials of Succoth refuse to feed Gideon
	10-12	Soldiers of Zebah and Zalmunna panic
	13-17	Gideon kills the men of the city
	18-21	Gideon kills Zebah and Zalmunna
	22-28	Gideon refuses to be king
	29-32	Gideon dies
	33-35	Israelites serve the Baals
9:1-6		Abimelech made king at Shechem
	7-21	Jotham's parable of the bramble
	22-33	Men plan to overthrow Abimelech
	34-45	Abimelech stops the men
	46-49	Abimelech burns the Tower of Shechem
	50-57	Abimelech dies in battle
10:1-5		Tola and Jair judge Israel
	6-9	Philistines capture the Israelites
	10-17	Israelites cry to God
11:1-11		Israelites appeal to Jephthah

	12-28	Jephthah and the Ammonite king
	29-33	Jephthah's vow
	34-40	Jephthah sacrifices his daughter
12:1-7		Jephthah quarrels with Ephraim
	8-15	Ibzan, Eton and Abdon judge Israel
	13:1	
13:2-7		Manoah will have a son
	8-20	Manoah and the angel of the Lord
	21-25	Manoah's wife bears Samson
14:1-9		Samson and the woman of Timnah
	10-20	Samson's riddle at his wedding
15:1-8		Samson slaughters some Philistines
	9-20	Samson defeats more Philistines
16:1-3		Samson steals the city gates
	4-9	Delilah seeks Samson's secret
	10-14	Delilah's second and third attempts
	15-17	Secret of Samson's strength
	18-22	Philistines capture and imprison Samson
	23-31	Samson revenges on the Philistines
17:1-13		Micah's idols and priest
18:1-13		Report of the Danite spies
	14-26	Danite men seize Micah's idols and priests
	27-31	Danites burn Laishites, then rebuild their city
19:1-9		Levite and his concubine
	10-21	Levites spend the night at Gibe-ah
	22-30	Base men abuse the concubine
20:1-11		Israelites hear about the abuse
	12-17	Benjamites muster their men
	18-28	Benjamites win twice
	29-48	Israelites rout the Benjaminites
21:1-7		Israelites weep for the Benjaminites
	8-15	Israelites attack Jabesh-gilead
	16-25	Wives for the Benjaminites

RUTH		**History/Early Prophets**
1:1-5		Elimelech stays in Moab and dies there
	6-14	Naomi decides to return home
	15-22	Ruth refuses to leave Naomi
2:1-7		Ruth gleans in the field
	8-16	Boaz provides for Ruth
	17-23	Namoi recognizes Boaz as kin

3:1-13		Naomi visits Boaz
	14-18	Boaz gives grain to Ruth
4:1-9		Boaz buys Naomi's land
	10-12	Boaz becomes Boaz's wife
	13-17	Ruth bears Obed
	18-22	Perez's descendants

1 SAMUEL **History/Early Prophets**

1:1-20		Hannah bears Samuel
	21-28	Hannah dedicates Samuel to God
2:1-11		Hannah's song of praise
	12-17	Custom of the priests
	18-26	Samuel ministers before the Lord
	27-36	Prophecy of doom to Eli
3:1-9		Lord calls Samuel
	10-21	God to punish Eli's family
4:1-11		Philistines defeat the Israelites
	12-22	Eli falls on his neck and dies
5:1-12		Philistines capture the ark
6:1-9		Plans to return the ark
	10-21;	Philistines return the ark
	7:1-2	
7:3-4		Samuel calls Israelites to repentance
	5-11	Israelites defeat the Philistines
	12-17	Ebenezer stone
8:1-9		Israelites demand a king
	10-22	God warns of the ways of a king
9:1-14		Saul comes to Samuel
	15-27	Saul and Samuel talk
10:1-8		Samuel anoints Saul
	9-16	Saul among the prophets
	17-27	Saul becomes king of Israel
	11:1-15	Israelites defeat the Ammonites
12:1-5		Samuel speaks to the Israelites
	6-25	Saving deeds of the Lord
13:1-7		Israelites battle the Philistines
	8-15	Saul offers by fire to the Lord
	16-23	Saul's six hundred warriors
14:1-15		Jonathan attacks the Philistines
	16-23	Philistines flee
	24-35	Jonathan breaks Saul's oath

	36-42	Jonathan proves guilty
	43-46	People save Jonathan
	47-52	Saul battles his enemies
15:1-9		Israelites battle the Amalekites
	10-16	Saul disobeys God
	17-23	Samuel delivers the Lord's sentence
	24-35	Saul appears to repent
16:1-5		Samuel sacrifices to the Lord
	6-13	God chooses David to be king
	14-23	David plays the lyre for Saul
17:1-11		Goliath the Philistine
	12-30	David goes to the battlefield
	31-40	David prepares to meet Goliath
	41-49	David challenges Goliath
	50-58	David kills Goliath; the Philistines flee
18:1-5		David and Jonathan become friends
	6-19	Saul hates David
	20-30	David marries Saul's daughter
19:1-7		Jonathan tries to pacify Saul
	8-10	Saul tries to kill David
	11-17	Michal helps David escape
	18-24	Saul prophesies
20:1-11		David and Jonathan meet at Naioth
	12-23	Covenant of David and Jonathan
	24-29	Jonathan's excuse for David
	30-42	Saul wants to kill David
21:1-7		Ahimelech and the holy bread
	8-15	David escapes to Gath
22:1-10		David continues to flee
	11-23	Saul sends servants to kill Ahimelech
23:1-14		David at Keilah
	15-18	David and Jonathan's covenant
	19-29	Ziphites betray David
24:1-15		David spares Saul
	16-22	Saul appears to repent
25:1-13		David asks Nabal for food
	14-22	Abigail hears that Nabal refuses
	23-35	Abigail pacifies David
	36-43	Nabal dies
26:1-5		Ziphites betray David again
	6-16	David spares Saul again

	17-25	Saul apologizes to David
27:1-7		David lives with the Philistines
	8-12	David raids many foreigners
28:1-2		David serves as Aehsh's bodyguard
	3-14	Saul and the medium at Endor
	15-25	Demon talks like Saul
29:1-11		Philistines dismiss David
30:1-6		Amalekites raid Ziklag
	7-15	David consults the ephod
	16-31	David slaughters the Amalekites
31:1-13		Saul falls on his own sword

2 SAMUEL   History/Early Prophets

1:1-16		David hears that Saul is dead
	17-27	David laments
2:1-7		God anoints David king over Judah
	8-17	Ish-bosheth, king of Israel
	18-23	Abner kills Asahel
	24-32	Abner and Joab declare a truce
3:1-16		Abner and Ish-bosheth quarrel
	17-25	Abner visits David
	26-39	Joab kills Abner
4:1-12		Rechab and Baanah slay Ish-bosheth
5:1-5		Israelites anoint David as their king
	6-16	David and his men capture Jerusalem
	17-25	David defeats the Philistines
6:1-11		David's men bring the ark to Jerusalem
	12-19	David dances before the Lord
	20-23	Michal rebukes David
7:1-17		Nathan delivers the prophecy to David
	18-29	David's prayer
8:1-18		David captures many foreigners
9:1-13		David acts kind to Mephibosheth
10:1-5		Ammonites mistreat David's ambassadors
	6 -14	Syrians and Ammonites flee
	15-19	David conquers the Ammonites
11:1-13		David's sin against Uriah
	14-25	David assigns Uriah to die
	26-27	David marries Bathsheba
12:1-6		Nathan's parable
	7-15	David repents

	16-23	David and Bathsheba's child dies
	24-25	Bathsheba bears Soloman
	26-31	Joab conquers the Ammonites
13:1-14		Amnon defiles Tamar
	15-22	Tamar cries aloud and mourns
	23-33	Absalom murders Amnon
	34-39	Absalom flees to Geshur
14:1-24		Joab brings back Absalom
	25-33	Absalom lives in Jerusalem
15:1-12		Absalom rebels against David
	13-23	David and his housemembers flee
	24-29	Zadok and the Levites return the ark
	30-37	Ahithopel conspires with Absalom
16:1-4		Ziba's lie
	5-14	Shime-i curses David
	15-23	Absalom comes to Jerusalem
17:1-4		Ahithopel advises to muster troops
	5-16	Counsel of Hushai
	17-23	Jonathan and Ahima-az warn David
	24-29;	David musters his men
	18:1-5	
18:6-8		Men battle in Ephraim forest
	9-18	Joab kills Absalom
19:1-8		David learns Absalom's death; Joab's rebuke
	9-15	Elders invite David back
	16-23	David forgives Shime-i
	24-30	Mephibosheth explains
	31-40	David blesses Barzillai
	41-43	Israelites and Judeans argue
20:1-3		Sheba leads the Israelites to rebel
	4-13	Joab kills Amasa
	14-26	People kill Sheba
21:1-9		Gibeonites hang seven Israelites
	10-14	David reburies Saul's and Jonathan's bones
	15-22	David wins wars against the Philistines
22:1-51		David's psalm of praise
23:1-7		David's last words
	8-39	Deeds of David's mighty men
24:1-9		Joab counts the Israelites and Judeans
	10-14	David faces a choice
	15-25	Lord sends then averts plague upon Israelites

1 KINGS		**History/Early Prophets**
1:1-4		David in old age
	5-14	Adonijah seeks to be king
	15-27	Bathsheba and Nathan
	28-37	David decides for Solomon
	38-53	Zadok anoints Solomon as king
2:1-12		David's last words
	13-25	Benaiah kills Adonijah
	26-35	Solomon expels Abiathar; Benaiah kills Joab
	36-46	Shime-i's broken oath; Benaiah kills Shime-I
3:1-2		Solomon's marriage pact with Pharaoh
	3-15	God grants Solomon wisdom
	16-28	Solomon's wise decision
4:1-21		Men of Solomon's court
	22-28	Household supplies
	29-34	Solomon is the wisest of all men
5:1-18		Solomon orders temple; forces men to build
6:1-37		Temple and its interior
7:1-12		Palace buildings
	13-22	Hiram works for Solomon
	23-39	Molten sea and brass lavers
	40-51	Other temple furniture
8:1-13		Leaders bring the ark to the temple
	14-21	Solomon's talk to the people
	22-53	Solomon's prayer of dedication
	54-61	Solomon praises the Lord
	62-66	Sacrifice and feast
9:1-9		Lord's covenant with Solomon
	10-28	Solomon forces men to build
10:1-13		Queen of Sheba visits
	14-29	Solomon's riches
11:1-8		Solomon marries foreign women
	9-13	Lord warns Solomon
	14-25	Solomon's enemies: Hadad and Rezon
	26-40	Abijah's prophecy about Jeroboam
	41-43	Solomon dies
12:1-11		Rehoboam, king of Israel
	12-20	Ten tribes rebel
	21-24	God's command to Rehoboam
	25-33	Jeroboam worships a calf
13:1-10		Prophecy about Josiah

	11-19	Lying prophet
	20-32	Lion kills the man of God
	33-34	Jeroboam continues to sin
14:1-16		Jeroboam's son Abijah to die
	17-20	Jeroboam dies
	21-31	Rehoboam, king of judah
15:1-8		Abijam, king of Judah
	9-15	Asa, king of Judah
	16-24	Judeans and Israelites war
	25-32	Nadab, king of Israel
	33-34;	Baasha, king of Israel
	16:1-7	
16:8-14		Elah, king of Israel
	15-20	Zimri, king of Israel
	21-28	Ornri, king of Israel
	29-34	Ahab, king of Israel
17:1-7		Ravens feed Elijah
	8-24	Elijah raises the widow's son
18:1-16		Elijah and Obadiah meet
	17-19	Elijah and Ahab meet
	20-29	Priests of Baal on Mount Carmel
	30-40	Fire consumes Elijah's sacrifice
	41-46	Great rain comes
19:1-8		Elijah flees from Jezebel
	9-18	Elijah in the mountain cave
	19-21	Elijah casts his mantle on Elisha
20:1-22		Ahab slaughters the Syrians
	23-30	Ahab again slaughters the Syrians
	31-34	Ahab spares Ben-hadad
	35-43	Prophet judges Ahab for sparing Ben-hadad
21: 1-4		Ahab covets Naboth's vineyard
	5-16	Jezebel seizes the vineyard
	17-26	Elijah announces doom
	27-29	Ahab repents
22:1-4		Ahab's pact with Jehoshaphat
	5-12	Lying prophets
	13-28	Micaiah, the true prophet
	29-40	Ahab dies in battle
	41-50	Jehoshaphat, king of Judah
	51-53	Ahaziah, king of Israel

2 KINGS		**History/Early Prophets**
1:1-8		Ahaziah inquires of Baal-zebub
	9-16	Kings men attempt to seize Elijah
	17-18	Jehoram, king of Israel
2:1-12		Lord takes Elijah up into heaven
	13-25	Elisha begins to perform miracles
3:1-19		Jehoram musters troops in Samaria
	13-20	Elisha assures Jehoram of victory
	21-27	Jehoram's campaign against Moab
4:1-7		Widow's jar of oil
	8-17	Shunammite woman to have son
	18-38	Elisha brings the son back to life
	38-41	Elisha makes poisonous food harmless
	42-44	One hundred men eat of Elisha's portion
5:1-14		Leprosy leaves Naaman
	15-19	Elisha refuses a reward
	20-27	Gehazi asks for money; Elisha punishes him
6:1-7		Elisha locates the lost axe head
	8-19	Elisha strikes the Syrians blind
	20-31	Elisha leads the blind Syrians to Samaria
	32-33;	Elisha's prophecy
	7:1-2	
7:3-15		Syrians flee
	16-20	Israelites plunder the Syrian camp
8:1-6		Shunammite woman comes home
	7-15	Hazael kills Ben-hadad; becomes Syrian king
	16-24	Jehoram, king of Judah
	25-29	Ahaziah, king of Judah
9:1-13		Jehu becomes king of Israel
	14-26	Jehu tricks and kills Joram
	27-29	Ahaziah flees but men kill him
	30-37	Men kill Jezebel
10:1-11		Ahab's seventy sons to be beheaded
	12-17	Jehu kills Ahaziah and Ahab's kin
	18-27	Jehu slaughters the Baal worshipers
	28-36	Summary of Jehu's reign
11:1-3		Athaliah, queen of Judah
	4-20	Jehoiada overthrows Athaliah
	21;	Jehoash, king of Judah
	12:1-3	
12:4-16		Jehoash repairs the temple

	17-21	Jehoash pays Hazael not to attack Judah
13:1-9		Jehoahaz, king of Israel
	10-13	Jehoash, king of Israel
	14-25	Elisha dies
14:1-14		Amaziah, king of Judah
	15-16	Jehoash dies
	17-22	Amaziah dies
	23-29	Jeroboaro II, king of Israel
15:1-7		Azariah, king of Judah
	8-12	Zechariah, king of Israel
	13-16	Shallum, king of Israel
	17-22	Menahem, king of Israel
	23-36	Pekahiah, king of Israel
	27-31	Pekah, king of Israel
	32-38	Jotham, king of Judah
16:1-20		Ahaz, king of Judah
17:1-6		Assyrians capture Samaria
	7-23	Israelites' and Judeans' sins
	24-34	Israelites resettle with Assyrians
	35-41	Serving the Lord but also graven images
18:1-8		Hezekiah, king of Judah
	9-12	Shalmaneser takes Israel to Assyria
	13-17	Hezekiah pays tribute to the Assyrians
	18-25	Shalmaneser threatens Israel once again
	26-37	The Rabshaken urges peace
19:1-13		Hezekiah sends his secretary to Isaiah
	14-19	Hezekiah's prayer
	20-34	Isaiah brings an answer
	35-37	Angel of the Lord slays the Assyrians
20:1-11		Hezekiah becomes sick and nearly dies
	12-21	Hezekiah shows envoys what he owns
21:1-9		Manasseh, king of Judah
	10-18	Prophets of God predict Jerusalem's fall
	19-26	Amon, kind of Judah
22:1-2		Josiah, king of Judah
	3-7	Josiah repairs the temple
	8-13	Book of the law
	14-20	Words of Huldah the Prophetess
23:1-3		Judeans renew the covenant with God
	4-14	Josiah's reforms
	15-20	Josiah destroys pagan altars and shrines

	21-27	People observe the Passover
	28-30	Josiah dies
	31-35	Jehoahaz, king of Judah
	36-37	Jehoiakim, king of Judah
24:1-7		Jehoiakim rebels and dies
	8-9	Jehoiachin, king of Judah
	10-17	King and his men surrender
	18-20; 25:1-7	Zedekiah reigns and besieges
25:8-21		Nebuchadnezzar destroys Jerusalem
	22-26	Men kill Gedaliah the governor
	27-30	Evil-merodach frees Jehoiachin

1 CHRONICLES   History/The Writings

1:1-42		Genealogies of the Patriarchal Age
	43-54	Kings of Edom
2:1-55		Genealogies from Israel
3:1-9		Family of David
	10-24	Family of Solomon
4:1-23		Family of Judah
	24-43	Family of Simeon
5:1-10		Family of Reuben
	11-22	Family of Gad
	23-26	Half-tribe of Manasseh
6:1-48		Family of Levi
	49-81	Family of Aaron
7:1-5		Family of Issachar
	6-12	Family of Benjamin
	13-19	Family of Naphtali
	20-29	Family of Ephraim
	30-40	Family of Asher
8:1-40		Family of Benjamin
9:1-34		Families that returned from Babylon
	35-44	Family of Saul
10:1-14		Saul's armor-bearer kills him
11:1-9		David, king of all Israel
	10-47	David's mighty men
12:1-22		David's supporters
	23-40	Number of David's armed men
13:1-14		People take the ark to Obed-edom
14:1-17		David defeats the Philistines

15:1-15		People prepare to move the ark
	16-24	Levites appoint men to play music
	25-29	David dances before the ark
16:1-6		Services and music
	7-36	David's psalm of gratitude
	37-43	Ministers and keepers of the ark
17:1-15		Nathan's warning to David
	16-27	David's prayer
18:1-17		David defeats many peoples
19:1-9		David and the Ammonites
	10-19	Syrians and the Ammonites flee
20:1-8		David defeats the Ammonites and Philistines
21:1-6		David counts the people
	7-17	God sends a plague
	18-30	Altar on Ornan's threshing floor
22:1-16		People prepare to build the temple
	17-19	David commands the leaders to help
23:1-23		David assembles the priests and the Levites
	24-32	Duties of the Levites
24:1-31		Division of the priests
25:1-31		David sets apart musicians for the service
26:1-19		David arranges for gatekeepers
	20-28	David arranges for treasuries
	29-32	Officers and judges
27:1-34		Military and civil officials
28:1-8		Officials to assist Solomon
	9-20	David's instructions to Solomon
29:1-9		David invites the people to give
	10-21	David's prayer
	22-25	Solomon reigns after David
	26-30	David dies
2 CHRONICLES		**History/The Writings**
1:1-17		Solomon asks the Lord for wisdom
2:1-18		Solomon plans to build the temple
3:1-17		Site, dimensions and materials
4:1-22;		Temple furniture
	5:1	
5:2-14		Levites bring the ark to the temple
6:1-11		Solomon speaks
	12-42	Solomon's prayer of dedication

7:1-10		Fire from heaven burns the offerings
	11-22	Lord's promise to Solomon
8:1-11		Solomon's buildings and cities
	12-18	Offering daily according to commands
9:1-12		Queen of Sheba visits
	13-28	Solomon's wealth and wisdom
	29-31	Solomon dies; Rehoboam becomes king
10:1-11		Rehoboam rules harshly
	12-19	Ten tribes revolt
11:1-12		Rehoboam erects fortresses
	13-17	Levites remain with Judah
	18-23	Rehoboam's many wives
12:1-12		Egyptians raid Jerusalem
	13-16	Summary of Rehoboam's reign
13:1-12		Abijah, king of Judah
	13-22	Abijah and Jeroboam war with each other
14:1-8		Asa, king of Judah
	9-15	Asa defeats Zerah
15:1-7		Prophet Azariah advises Asa
	8-19	Asa makes reforms
16:1-6		Asa allies with Ben-hadad
	7-10	Hanani the seer warns Asa
	11-14	Asa gets sick and dies
17:1-9		Jehoshaphat king of Judah
	10-19	Jehoshaphat's prosperity
18:1-3		Ahab bargains with Jehoshaphat
	4-11	Advice of the false prophets
	12-27	Micaiah's true prophetic message
	28-34	Warrior slays Ahab
19:1-22		Jehoshaphat makes reforms
20:1-12		Jehoshaphat's prayer
	13-19	Lord to deliver the people from Ammonites
	20-30	Lord delivers the people from Ammonites
	31-37	Jehoshaphat dies
21:1-10		Jehoram, king of Judah
	11-15	Elijah warns of a plague
	16-20	Jehoram dies
22:1-6		Ahaziah, king of Judah
	7-9	Jehu murders Ahaziah
	10-12	Athaliah murders the royal family
23:1-11		Jehoiada leads a revolt

	12-21	Athaliah dies
24:1-7		Joash, king of Judah
	8-14	Workmen restore the temple
	15-22	Jehoiada and his son die
	23-27	Servants slay Joash
25:1-16		Amaziah, king of Judah
	17-24	Judeans and Israelites war
	25-28	Murderers slay Amaziah
26:1-15		Uzziah, king of Judah
	16-23	Uzziah sins and dies
27:1-9		Jotham, king of Judah
28:1-4		Ahaz, king of Judah
	5-27	Syrians defeat Ahaz
29:1-2		Hezekiah, king of Judah
	3-11	Hezekiah cleanses the temple
	12-19	Levites sanctify the temple
	20-30	Hezekiah orders consecration of the temple
	31-36	Sacrifices in the temple
30:1-12		Hezekiah orders keeping of Passover
	13-27	People keep the Passover
31:1		Israelites destroy pagan altars
	2-10	Hezekiah appoints the Levitical divisions
	11-21	Things for the Levites
32:1-8		Hezekiah prepares to battle the Assyrians
	9-15	Sennacherib taunts Hezekiah
	16-23	Sennacherib's sons murder him
	24-33	Hezekiah becomes sick and dies
33:1-13		Manasseh, king of Judah
	14-20	Manasseh restores the altar
	21-25	Amon, king of Judah
34:1-7		Josiah, king of Judah
	8-13	Joaiah repairs the temple
	14-28	Hilkiah finds the book of the law
	29-33	Reading of the law
35:1-19		Preparing for and observing the Passover
	20-27	Josiah dies
36:1-16		Reign of Jehoahaz; people unfaithful
	17-21	Chaldeans defeat and exile the Israelites
	22-23	Cyrus promises end of exile

EZRA		**History/The Writings**
1:1-4		Cyrus proclaims the Israelites may return
	5-11	Israelites prepare to return
2:1-70		People returning with Zerubbabel
3:1-7		People rebuild the altar
	8-13	People begin to rebuild the temple
4:1-6		Judah's adversaries
	7-16	Letter to Artaxerxes
	17-24	King Artaxerxes stops the rebuilding
5:1-5		Zerubbabel begins to build the temple again
	6-17	Tattenai's letter to Darius
6:1-12		Darius searches and replies
	13-22	Elders finish and dedicate the temple
7:1-10		Ezra's genealogy and career
	11-28	Ezra's letter from Artaxerxes
8:1-14		People who are returning with Ezra
	15-20	Temple servants
	21-30	Ezra and the people prepare to return
	31-36	People arrive at Jerusalem
9:1-15		Ezra's prayer about marrying foreigners
10:1-8		Oath to put away foreign women
	9-17	People assemble in Jerusalem
	18-44	Priests who had foreign wives

NEHEMIAH		**History/The Writings**
1:1-11		Nehemiah's prayer for Israel
2:1-8		Nehemiah's request to go to Jerusalem
	9-16	Nehemiah inspects the walls
	17-20	Nehemiah determines to rebuild
3:1-32		Rebuilding begins
4:1-9		Plotting of Sanballat and Tobiah
	10-23	People station behind the wall
5:1-13		Complaint about poverty and famine
	14-19	Nehemiah's frugal diet
6:1-14		False rumors about Nehemiah
	15-19	Completion of the wall
7:1-4		Appointment of Hanani and Hananiah
	5-38	Genealogy of those who returned
	39-73	Priests and Levites who returned
	73; 8:1-12	Reading and explanation of the law

8:13-18		Celebration of the Feast of Booths
9:1-5		Separating from foreigners
	6-25	Ezra's prayer
	26-37	God's people rebel
	38;	Those who signed the covenant
	10:1-27	
10:28-39		Summary of the covenant
11:1-2		Reinhabitation of Jeruslem
	3-24	People living in Jerusalem
	25-36	Villages outside Jerusalem
12:1-26		Genealogies of priests and Levites
	27-43	Dedication of the city walls
	44-47	Collectors, singers and gatekeepers
13:1-3		Separation of foreigners from Israelites
	4-9	Nehemiah casts out Tobiah's furniture
	10-14	Support system for the priests begins
	15-22	Sabbath reforms begin
	23-30	Nehemiah: no marriage to foreign women

ESTHER   History/The Writings

1:1-9		Riches and splendor of Ahasu-erus
	10-22	Ahasu-erus removes Queen Vashti
2:1-4		Search for a queen
	5-11	Esther's background
	12-18	Ahasu-erus chooses Esther
	19-23	Plot to kill Ahasu-erus fails
3:1-6		Ahasu-erus promotes Haman
	7-11	Haman's plot against the Jews
	12-15;	Decree to kill the Jews
	4:1-3	
4:4-17		Mordecai asks Esther for help
5:1-8		Esther intervenes
	9-14	Haman has gallows made
6:1-14		Haman's plot and its failure
7:1-10		Downfall of Haman
8:1-2		Esther promotes Mordecai
	3-8	Esther's request
	9-14	Ahasu-erus revokes the decree
	15-17;	Victory of the Jews
	9:1-10	
9:11-15		Ahasu-erus hangs Haman's ten sons

	16-28	Feast of Purim
	29-32	Approval of Esther
10:1-3		Power and might of Mordecai

JOB		**Poetry/The Writings**
1:1-5		Job and his background
	6-12	God permits Satan to tempt Job
	13-22	Satan destroys Job's children & possessions
2:1-6		Satan's second request of God
	7-10	Satan afflicts Job with sores
	11-13	Job's friends
3:1-10		Job curses the day of his birth
	11-19	Job asks why he did not die
	20-26	Job cries out in his agony
4:1-11		Eliphaz gives a talk
	12-21	Can man or angels be pure before God?
5:1-7		Who can help man in trouble?
	8-16	God helps the man in trouble
	17-27	God will deliver from trouble
6:1-13		Job wants God to let him die
	14-23	Job calls his friends unfaithful
	24-30	Job wants to know where he has erred
7:1-6		Job's days end without hope
	7-15	Job loathes his life
	16-21	Job asks God to show him his sin
8:1-22		Bildad says God will reward the righteous
9:1-12		Job asks, "Who can hinder God?"
	13-24	Job claims innocence
	25-35	Job's complaint against God
10:1-13		Job asks God why He is punishing him
11:1-6		Zophar accuses Job of guilt
	7-12	Zophar talks of God's understanding
	13-20	Zophar urges Job to repent
12:1-6		Job denies Zophar's accusations
	7-12	Job describes God's power & understanding
	13-25	God's wisdom and might
13:1-12		Job says his friends' advice is worthless
	13-28	Job defends his integrity
14:1-6		Job talks of the frailty of man
	7-22	If a man dies, shall he live again?
15:1-16		Eliphaz says Job's own mouth condemns him

45

	17-35	End of an evil man
16:1-5		Job calls his friends miserable comforters
	6-17	Job's condition; Job claims purity
	18-22; 17:1-2	God is witness in Heaven
17:3-16		Job asks, "Where is my hope?"
18:1-4		Bildad reproves Job
	5-21	Misery of the wicked
19:1-7		Words of Job's friends torment him
	8-12	Job says God caused his afflictions
	13-24	Friends and family desert Job
	25-29	Faith in the living Redeemer
20:1-19		Zophar's talk on the wicked
	20-29	Zophar talks about the heritage of the wicked
21:1-16		Job talks about the prosperity of the wicked
	17-26	Job talks about the calamity of the wicked
	27-34	Job says the wicked prosper
22:1-11		Eliphaz accuses Job again
	12-20	Way of wicked men
	21-30	Eliphaz urges Job to return to God
23:1-17		Job wants to find God and be tried
24:1-12		Job describes the wicked
	13-25	Job says God supports the wicked
25:1-6		Bildad asks, "How can man be clean?"
26:1-14		Job asserts God's greatness
27:1-6		Job says his lips speak not wickedness
	7-12	Job despises the wicked
	13-23	Frustration of the wicked
28:1-11		Men search for gold and silver
	12-22	Where is wisdom and understanding?
	23-28	Fear of the Lord is wisdom
29:1-25		Job describes and longs for his prosperity
30:1-15		Job speaks of his mockers and haters
	16-31	Job talks about his turmoil
31:1-12		Job claims innocence of adultery and deceit
	13-28	Job's concern for the slave and the needy
	29-40	Job's concern for the enemy and the stranger
32:1-22		Elihu says he will declare his opinion
33:1-18		Elihu says Job is not right
	19-33	God chastens men to save them from the Pit
34:1-15		God will not do wickedly

	16-30	Elihu speaks of the power of God
	31-37;	Elihu says Job adds rebellion to sin
35:1-16		God does not hear the empty cry of sinners
36:1-16		God gives the afflicted their right
	17-23	Elihu's warning to Job
	24-33;	Praise the work of God
	37:1-13	
37:14-24		Consider His wondrous works
38:1-38		Lord tells Job of His power
	39-41	Wonders of animal life
	39:1-30	
	40:1-2	
40:3-14		Lord tells Job to abase the proud
	15-24	Strength of the Behemoth
41:1-34		Power of the Leviathan
42:1-6		Job repents in dust and ashes
	7-9	Eliphaz, Bildad, Zophar offer bulls and rams
	10-17	Lord restores Job's prosperity

PSALMS — **Poetry/The Writings**

1:1-3		Blessed and prosperous is the Godly man
	4-6	"The wicked will perish"
2:1-6		Why do peoples conspire against the Lord?
	7-12	Triumph of the Son
3:1-8		"Deliverance belongs to the Lord"
4:1-8		"Lord hears me when I call"
5:1-12		"For Thou dost bless the righteous"
6:1-10		Lord shall put my enemies to shame
7:1-17		"Save me from all my pursuers"
8:1-9		"Thou hast given him dominion over works"
9:1-20		"Thou has maintained my just cause"
10:1-11		When wicked men's ways prosper
	12-18	"Thou dost note trouble and grief"
11:1-7		"In the Lord I take refuge"
12:1-8		"Do Thou, O Lord, protect us?"
13:1-6		How long, O Lord, will Thou forget me?
14:1-7		Children of men have all gone astray
15:1-5		"Who shall dwell on Thy holy hill?"
16:1-11		"Thou dost show me the path of life"
17:1-9		"My steps have held fast to Thy paths"
	10-15	"Deliver my life from the wicked"

18:1-19		"He delivered me from my strong enemy"
	20-30	"According to my righteousness"
	31-50	"Triumphs He gives to His king"
19:1-14		"The law of the Lord is perfect"
20:1-9		"May He grant you your heart's desire"
21:1-13		"Thou hast given him his heart's desire"
22:1-21		"My God, why has Thou forsaken me"
	22-31	He has heard when the afflicted cried
23:1-6		"The Lord is my Shepherd"
24:1-10		"Who is the King of glory"
25:1-22		"O Lord, pardon my guilt"
26:1-12		"Vindicate my, O Lord"
27:1-14		"The Lord is my Light and my Salvation"
28:1-9		"I cry to Thee for help"
29:1-11		"The voice of the Lord"
30:1-12		"I will extol Thee, O Lord"
31:1-13		"Thou art my Rock and my Fortress"
	14-24	"My times are in Thy hand"
32:1-11		"I acknowledged my sin to Thee"
33:1-22		"Let all the earth fear the Lord"
34:1-22		"The Lord redeems the life of His servants"
35:1-16		"Contend with those who contend with me"
	17-28	"Bestir Thyself, and awaken for my right"
36:1-12		"For with Thee is the fountain of life"
37:1-11		"Trust in the Lord and do good"
	12-22	"the wicked perish"
	23-40	"The righteous shall possess the land"
38:1-14		"My wounds grow foul and fester"
	15-22	"Do not forsake me, O Lord"
39:1-13		"Lord, let me know my end"
40:1-10		"I delight to do Thy will, O my God"
	11-17	"Be pleased, O Lord, to deliver me"
41:1-13		"O Lord, be gracious to me"
42:1-11		"Why are you cast down, O my soul"
	43:1-5	
44:1-8		"Thou hast saved us from our foes"
	9-16	"Yet Thou hast cast us off"
	17-26	"Rise up, come to our help"
45:1-17		King's marriage
46:1-11		"God of Jacob is our Refuge"
47:1-9		"Sing praises to God, sing praises"

48:1-14		Song to Mount Zion
49:1-20		"Man cannot abide in his pomp"
50:1-23		"He who brings thanksgiving as his sacrifice"
51:1-19		"Create in me a clean hear, O God"
52:1-9		"God will break you down for ever"
53:1-6		"God will scatter the bones of the ungodly"
54:1-7		"Save me, O God, by Thy name"
55:1-15		"I am distraught by the noise of the enemy"
	16-23	"But Thou, O God, wilt cast them down"
56:1-13		"In God I trust without a fear"
57:1-11		God will send forth His faithfulness
58:1-11		"O God, break the teeth in their mouths"
59:1-17		"Deliver me from my enemies"
60:1-12		"Give victory by Thy right hand & answer us!"
61:1-8		"When my heart is faint"
62:1-7		"For God alone my soul waits in silence"
	8-12	"God is a Refuge for us"
63:1-11		"My soul thirsts for Thee"
64:1-10		"Preserve my life from dread of the enemy"
65:1-8		Hope and strength of God
	9-13	"The river of God is full of water"
66:1-7		"How terrible are Thy deeds"
	8-12	"For Thou, O God, hast tested us"
	13-20	"But truly God has listened"
67:1-7		"Let the peoples praise Thee, O God"
68:1-6		"Sing to God, sing praises to His name"
	7-10	"Thou didst march through the wilderness"
	11-14	"Kings of the armies, they flee! They flee!"
	15-18	"Thou hast ascended on high"
	19-23	"God is our Salvation"
	24-35	"Terrible is God in His sanctuary"
69:1-12		"The flood sweeps over me"
	13-21	"Let not the flood sweep over me"
	22-28	"Let their eyes be darkened"
	29-36	"God will save Zion"
70:1-5		"Thou art my Help and my Deliverer"
71:1-24		"Do not cast me off in the time of old age"
72:1-20		Prayer for the king
73:1-20		End of the wicked
	21-28	"God is the Strength of my heart"
74:1-23		"How long, O God, is the foe to scoff?"

75:1-10		"I will judge with equity"
76:1-12		"Glorious art Thou"
77:1-10		"I cry aloud to God"
	11-20	"Thou art the God who workest wonders"
78:1-8		"Give ear, O my people, to my law"
	9-16	God's miracles
	17-31	"Bread of the angels"
	32-39	"He restrained His anger"
	40-55	Plagues for the Egyptians
	56-66	"He gave His people over to the sword"
	67-72	"Israel His inheritance"
79:1-13		Lament of the destruction of Jerusalem
80:1-19		"Restore us, O God"
81:1-16		"Hear, O my people, while I admonish you!"
82:1-8		"How long will you judge unjustly?"
83:1-18		"Let them be put to shame"
84:1-12		My soul longs for the courts of the Lord
85:1-13		"Wilt Thou not revive us again?"
86:1-17		"Give ear, O Lord, to my prayer"
87:1-7		"Glorious things are spoke of Thee"
88:1-18		"My soul is full of troubles'
89:1-4		"I have sworn to David"
	5-18	"Thou hast a might arm"
	19-37	God's promises to David
	38-52	Plea for renewal of the covenant
90:1-12		Eternal God and mortal man
	13-17	"Have pity on Thy servants"
91:1-16		"I will deliver him"
92:1-15		"How great are Thy works, O Lord"
93:1-5		"He is robed in majesty"
94:1-23		Thou God of vengeance, shine forth"
95:1-11		"Let us sing to the Lord"
96:1-13		"Declare His glory among the nations"
97:1-12		Power and dominion of the Lord
98:1-9		"O sing to the Lord a new song"
99:1-9		The Lord is great and holy
100:1-5		"Serve the Lord with gladness!"
101:1-8		"I will sing of loyalty and of justice"
102:1-11		"My days pass away like smoke"
	12-22	The Lord will build up Zion
	23-28	God's years and man's days

103:1-14		"Forget no all His benefits"
104:1-13		"O Lord, how manifold are Thy works!"
105:1-22		"He is mindful of His Covenant forever"
	23-36	"Then Israel came to Egypt"
	37-45	"Then He led forth Israel"
106:1-5		"Remember me, O Lord"
	6-12	Israelites' sins at the Red Sea
	13-18	Israelites' sins in the wilderness
	19-23	Golden calf at Horeb
	24-39	Israelites' sins in Canaan
	40-48	Israelites' punishment; God's mercy
107:1-3		"Whom He has redeemed from trouble"
	4-16	"Some wandered, some sat in darkness"
	17-22	"Some were sick"
	23-32	"Some went down to the sea"
	33-43	"By His blessing they multiply"
108:1-13		"My heart is steadfast, O God"
109:1-5		"They beset me with words of hate"
	6-19	Curses upon the wicked
	20-31	"Help me, O Lord my God"
110:1-7		"The Lord is at your right hand"
111:1-10		"Great are the works of the Lord"
112:1-10		"Blessed is the man who fears the Lord"
113:1-9		"Praise the Lord!"
114:1-8		"When Israel went out of Egypt"
115:1-18		"He is their Help and their Shield"
116:1-19		"I called on the name of the Lord"
117:1-2		"The faithfulness of the Lord endures forever"
118:1-9		"His mercy endures forever"
	10-14	"They surround me like bees"
	15-20	"The right hand of the Lord does valiantly"
	21-29	"The Stone which the builders rejected"
119:1-8		"Blessed are those whose way is blameless?
	9-16	"How can a young man keep his way pure?"
	17-24	"Open my eyes that I may behold"
	25-48	"Teach me Thy statutes"
	49-56	"They statutes have been my songs"
	57-64	"I promise to keep Thy words"
	65-72	"It is good for me that I was afflicted"
	73-80	"Let Thy mercy come to me"
	81-88	"I hope in Thy word"

	89-96	"Thy word is firmly fixed in the heavens"
	97-104	"Oh, how I love Thy law!"
	105-112	"Thy word is a lamp to my feet"
	113-120	"Thou art my Hiding Place"
	121-128	"I have done what is right and just"
	129-136	"Keep steady my steps"
	137-144	"Thy word is very pure"
	145-152	"With my whole heart I cry"
	153-160	"I do not forget Thy law"
	161-168	"I rejoice at Thy word"
	169-176	"Deliver me according to Thy word"
120:1-7		"In my distress I cry to the Lord"
121:1-8		"The Lord is your Keeper"
122:1-9		"Pray for the peace of Jerusalem"
123:1-4		"Have mercy upon us, O Lord"
124:1-8		"If it had not been the Lord"
125:1-5		"Those who trust in the Lord"
126:1-6		"Restore our fortunes, O Lord"
127:1-5		"Unless the Lord builds the house"
128:1-6		The man who fears the Lord shall be blessed
129:1-8		"Many a time have they afflicted me"
130:1-8		"I wait for the Lord"
131:1-3		"O Lord, my heart is not lifted up"
132:1-10		David and the ark of the Lord
	11-18	"The Lord swore to David a sure oath"
133:1-3		"When brothers dwell in unity!"
134:1-3		Blessing for the night servants
135:1-7		"Praise the Lord, for the Lord is good"
	8-14	"He is was who smote"
	15-21	Scorn of idols
136:1-9		God's wonders of creation
	10-26	God's deliverance of His people from Egypt
137:1-9		"By the waters of Babylon"
138:1-8		"All the kings of the earth shall praise Thee"
139:1-18		"O Lord, Thou hast searched me"
	19-24	"I count them my enemies"
140:1-13		"Preserve me from violent men"
141:1-10		"Let not my heart incline to evil"
142:1-7		"Bring me out of prison"
143:1-12		"For Thy name's sake, O Lord, preserve my life!"

144:1-15		"My Stronghold and my Deliverer"
145:1-13		"I will extol Thee, my God and King"
	14-21	"The Lord is faithful in all His words"
146:1-10		"Put not your trust in princes"
147:1-20		Might and grace of the Lord
148:1-14		Call for nature to praise the Lord
149:1-9		"The Lord takes pleasure in His people"
150:1-6		"Praise the Lord!"

PROVERBS — **Poetry/The Writings**

1:1-9		Proverbs provide wisdom
	10-19	Warnings against violence
	20-33	Warning against neglect of wisdom
2:1-15		Reward of wisdom
	16-22	To deliver you from the loose woman
3:1-4		Let not loyalty forsake you
	5-8	Trust in the Lord
	9-10	Honor the Lord with your substance
	11-12	Do not despise the Lord's discipline
	13-20	Wisdom exceeds wealth in value
	21-35	Wise inherit honor, fools get disgrace
4:1-9		Command to obtain wisdom
	10-19	Contrast of the wise and the wicked
	20-27	Attend my words, heed your path
5:1-14		Keep away from the loose woman
	15-23	Rejoice in the wife of your youth
6:1-11		Warnings against pledges and sluggards
	12-15	Warning against sowing discord
	16-19	Warning against seven sins
	20-35	Warning against adultery
7:1-27		Folly of yielding to the loose woman
8:1-21		Call of wisdom
	22-31	Eternity of wisdom
	32-36	Happy is the man who listens to wisdom
9:1-6		Wisdom has built her house
	7-12	IF you reprove a scoffer
	13-18	A foolish woman is noisy
10:1-22		A wise son; a slack hand; tongue of righteous
	23-32	Fear of the Lord prolongs life
11:1-11		False balance; pride; blessing of the upright
	12-23	Gracious woman; kind vs. wicked man

	24-31	One man gives freely; fruit of the righteous
12:1-8		Whoever loves discipline; righteous' thoughts
	9-14	Care for life of your beast and land
	15-28	Truth; deceit; lying lips; diligence
13:1-11		Fruit of the mouth; wealth
	12-25	Desire fulfilled; prudent man; inheritance
14:1-19		Talk of a fool; lips of the wise; laughter
	20-35	Rich and the poor; wisdom; fear of the Lord
15:1-12		A soft answer; tongue of the wise
	13-20	Reward of a cheerful heart
	21-33	Wise man's path; mind of the righteous
16:1-11		Lord weighs the way of man
	12-24	Wisdom the fountain of life
	25-33	Wicked ways of men
17:1-12		Fine talk and false talk
	13-28	Beginnings of strife; a stupid son
18:1-16		Words of wise and foolish; humility; wealth
	17-24	Deciding disputes; power of the tongue; wife
19:1-17		Wealth and poverty; false witness
	18-29	Advice; instruction; loyalty; sluggard; scoffer
20:1-14		Wine; strife; sluggard; diverse weights
	15-30	Lips of knowledge; surety; gossiping
21:1-12		Haughty eyes; contentious woman
	13-31	Cry of the poor; scoffer; sluggard
22:1-16		Riches and honor; child; scoffer; sluggard
	17-29	Words of the wise; poor; pledges; skilful man
23:1-14		Delicacies; wealth; discipline
	15-35; 24:1-2	Wise words to a son; drunkard; glutton; harlot
24:3-12		Wisdom; stumbling to the slaughter
	13-22	Counsel to son; enemy; evildoers
	23-34	Sayings of wise; partiality; witness; sluggard
25:1-14		Glory of God;' king' court' word fitly spoken
	15-28	Honey; neighbors house; heavy heart
26:1-12		Fool and his folly
	13-28	Lazy man and the lying tongue
27:1-16		Tomorrow; praise; faithful wounds of a friend
	17-27	Iron sharpens iron; eyes of man; flocks
28:1-28		Poor man; wicked ruler; faithful man
29:1-27		When the righteous rule; discipline
30:1-14		Word of God; slander; curse

	15-33	Four things
31:1-9		Folly of lust and strong drink
	10-31	Virtuous woman

ECCLESIASTES — Poetry/The Writings

1:1-11		All is vanity
	12-18	In much wisdom is much vexation
2:1-11		Vanity of pleasure and wealth
	12-17	Wise man dies just like the fool
	18-23	Vanity of toil
	24-26	Food and enjoyment from God
3:1-9		For everything there is a season
	10-15	God gives beauty and pleasure
	16-22;	Man has no advantage over beasts
4:1-3		No one to comfort the oppressed
	4-6	Toil of the wise and the foolish
	7-12	Two are better than one
	13-16	Better is a poor and wise youth
5:1-7		Be not rash with your mouth
	8-17	Vanity of riches; man who lost his riches
	18-20	Enjoyment in toil is a gift of God
6:1-6		Vanity of wealth and honor
	7-12	Vanity of man's life
7:1-9		Choosing the better
	10-14	Value of wisdom over wealth
	15-18	Advice to be temperate
	19-29	The search for the sum of things
8:1-9		Keep the king's command
	10-13	It will not be well with the wicked
	14-17	The wise cannot know all the works of God
9:1-6		One fate comes to all
	7-10	What your hand finds to do, do it with might
	11-12	Time and chance happen to all
	13-17	Poor, wise man saved a city
10:1-15		Wise man and the fool
	16-20	King and the princes
11:1-8		Cast your bread upon the waters
	9-10	Rejoice, O young man
12:1-8		Remember the Creator before evil days come
	9-14	Fear God, keep His commandments

SONG OF SONGS		**Poetry/The Writings**
1:1-4		"The king has brought me into his chambers"
	5-6	Maiden is dark but comely
	7	"Where do you pasture your flock?"
	8	"Follow in the tracks of the flock"
	9-11	Ornaments for the maiden
	12-17; 2:1-2	"Behold, you are beautiful, my love"
2:3-7		Beloved like an apple tree
	8-17	Maiden's beloved appears
3:1-5		Maiden brings beloved to her mother's house
	6-11	King Solomon is returning
4:1-7		Description of the maiden
	8-15	"Come with me from Lebanon, my bride"
	16	"Let my beloved come to his garden"
5:1		"I come to my garden"
	2-8	Beloved comes then goes
	9	"What is your beloved more than another?"
	10-16	Description of the beloved
6:1		"Whither is they beloved gone?"
	2-3	Beloved is in his garden
	4-10	Description of the maiden
	11-12	Maiden in the nut garden
	13	"Return, return, O Shulammite"
7:1-9		Description of the maiden
	10-13	Maiden offers to give love in vineyards
8:1-4		"I would lead you to my mother's house"
	5-7	Strength of love
	8-1o	"We have a little sister"
	11-12	My vineyard
	13-14	"Hear your voice" "Make haste my beloved"
ISAIAH		**Prophets/Major Prophets**
1:1-9		Israelites continue to rebel
	10-17	God's requirement of a holy life
	18-31	Redemption or destruction
2:1-4		God's Kingdom will triumph on earth
	5-11	Land contains diviners, soothsayers, idols
	12-22	Proud will be humbled
3:1-12		Women and babes will rule
	13-26;	Lord will punish the daughters of Zion

	4:1	
4:2-6		Blessings the Messiah will provide
5:1-7		Parable of the vineyard
	8-23	Guilt of the Judeans
	24-30	God's judgment against the Judeans
6:1-5		Isaiah sees the Lord of Hosts
	6-13	Isaiah's commission
7:1-9		Isaiah's words to Ahaz
	10-25	Sign of Immanuel
8:1-15		War to come and the deliverer
	16-22	Command to trust the Lord
9:1-7		The Prince of Peace to come
	8-17	Ephraimite's pride and hypocrisy
	18-21	Destructive power of sin
10:1-4		Woe to the lawmakers of oppression
	5-19	Assyria, the rod, will be destroyed
	20-34	Remnant of the Israelites will be saved
11:1-9		Branch from the root of Jesse
	10-16	Messiah will restore Israel
12:1-6		Thanksgiving for God's salvation
13:1-8		Oracle about the doom of Babylon
	9-16	Coming Day of the Lord
	17-22	Medes will overthrow Babylon
14:1-23		Taunting the king of Babylon
	24-27	Lord will break the Assyrian
	28-32	Oracle about Philistia
15:1-9		Moab will be devastated
16:1-14		Moabites pride and fall
17:1-8		Crushing Damascus and Ephraim
	9-14	Horrors of invasion
18:1-7		Oracle about Ethiopia
19:1-17		Doom of Egypt
	18-25	Egyptians and Assyrians worship the Lord
20:1-6		Egypt will be conquered by Assyrians
21:1-10		Elamites and Medians defeat Babylonians
	11-17	Oracles about Dumah and Arabia
22:1-14		Oracle about Jerusalem
	15-25	Oracle against Shebna
23:1-18		Oracle about Tyre
24:1-16		Judgment for universal sinning
	17-23;	Reign of the Lord

	25:1-5	
25:6-12		Mountain of the Lord will be blessed
26:1-15		Song of rejoicing in Judah
	16-21	Hope in resurrection
27:1-13		Israelites will be delivered
28:1-8		Woe upon the drunkards of Ephraim
	9-22	Scoffers will be scourged by Assyrians
	23-29	Parable of the farmer
29:1-8		Doom to the city of Jerusalem
	9-16	Folly of trying to deceive
	17-24	God's people will be delivered
30:1-7		Sinfully relying upon Egyptians
	8-17	Rebellious Judeans will be crushed
	18-26	God's promise to the repentant
	27-33	Israelites' enemies will be smitten
31:1-5		Folly of relying upon the Egyptians
	6-9	Call to trust in the Lord
32:1-8		Israelites will be delivered
	9-20	After calamity, restoration
33:1-6		Destruction of the treacherous
	7-16	Judeans' distress; God's vengeance
	17-24	Joy the Messiah will give
34:1-4		Lord will destroy the peoples
	5-17	Example of the Edomites
35:1-10		God promises return to Zion
36:1-10		Sennacherib taunts Hezekiah
	11-22	Summons to surrender
37:1-7		Hezekiah's appeal to God
	8-13	Assyrians challenge
	14-20	Hezekiah's prayer to the Lord
	21-29	Promise of deliverance
	30-38	God fulfills His promise
38:1-8		Hezekiah's prayer while sick
	9-21	Hezekiah praises God after he recovers
39:1-8		Hezekiah's folly and exile
40:1-11		Messenger of the Lord will come
	12-17	God's power and wisdom
	18-26	Idols and the living God in contrast
	27-31	Everlasting God
41:1-7		Judging the peoples
	8-10	Israelites are chosen of God

	11-16	Israelites will overcome their foes
	17-20	God will prosper the Israelites
	21-29	God able to foretell the future
42:1-4		Mission of God's servant
	5-9	Servant like a light to the peoples
	10-13	Song of praise to the Lord
	14-17	Promise of destruction
	18-25	Peoples' sin and how God punishes then
43:1-7		God's love will redeem His people
	8-13	People chosen as a witness
	14-21	Redeemer to restore His people
	22-28	Israelites' sin of ingratitude
44:1-5		How God blesses the people
	6-8	God asks, "Who is like me?"
	9-20	God's opinion of idols and idolators
	21-28	Some things the Lord has done
45:1-8		Cyrus will restore Jerusalem
	9-13	Folly of striving with God
	14-19	Gentiles will be converted
	20-25	Lord offers peoples salvation
46:1-13		Babylon's idols and the Lord
47:1-7		Judging the Babylonians
	8-15	Babylonians are falsely secure
48:1-11		What God declares comes to pass
	12-16	Lord shall perform against Babylonians
	17-22	Command to flee Babylon
49:1-7		Servant's call and commission
	8-13	God cares for His redeemed
	14-21	God will not forget Zion
	22-26	Israel will be gloriously restored
50:1-3		Sin separates the Israelites from God
	4-11	Obedient response of the Servant
51:1-11		Encouragement to trust in God
	12-16	Lord will deliver His people
	17-23	Israelites will be oppressed
52:1-6		God will restore Jerusalem
	7-12	Exultant response of the captives
	13-15	Servant will be exalted
53:1-3		Servant as man sees Him
	4-6	Servant as God sees Him
	7-12	His death as man sees it; as God see it

54:1-17		Blessings the Servant will provide
55:1-5		Great call to follow God
	6-13	Lord pardons abundantly
56:1-8		Foreigners will receive blessing
	9-12	Failure of the Israelites' leaders
57:1-13		God condemns idols
	14-21	God has compassion for the repentant
58:1-7		Right and wrong fasting
	8-14	Righteous will receive protection and blessing
59:1-8		Sin keeps the Israelites from deliverance
	9-15	Israelites acknowledge their sins
	16-22	God will redeem Zion
60:1-9		Zion's glory
	10-14	Supremacy of God's people
	15-22	Majesty of the new Zion
61:1-9		Good news of salvation
	10-11	All peoples to see righteousness
62:1-12		Zion will be restored and glorified
63:1-6		Year of redemption
	7-9	Israelites, the elect of God
	10-14	Mighty deeds of God
	15-19	Judeans appeal to God
64:1-7		Guilty in God's presence
	8-12	Desolation of Jerusalem
65:1-7		God will repay: for the Israelites' sins
	8-16	Righteous will be saved
	17-25	New heaven and earth
66:1-4		True and false worshipping
	5-14	Birth of a people
	15-17	Fire of judgment
	18-24	Peoples shall see God's glory
JEREMIAH		**Prophets/Major Prophets**
1:1-19		Jeremiah's call and commission
2:1-13		Israelites' faithlessness
	14-19	Consequence of apostasy
	20-28	Punishment for idolatry
	29-37	Israelites will be punished
3:1-5		Judeans, like an unfaithful wife
	6-20	Israelites, the faithless ones
	21-25;	Call to repentance

	4:1-4	
4:5-22		Evil from the north
	23-31	Extent of desolation
5:1-9		Not one upright man found
	10-17	Call to invade Judah
	18-31	God's reason for judgment
6:1-5		Call for faithful to flee
	6-15	Encouragement of besiegers
	16-21	People refuse to repent
	22-30	Invader will suddenly destroy
7:1-20		Judeans are idolatrous and immoral
	21-29	Israelites walk their own way
	30-34;	Terrible to come
	8:1-3	
8:4-21		Holding fast to deceit
	22;	Punishment for the unrepentant
	9:1-9	
9:10-22		Wailing over Jerusalem's ruin
	23-26	Glory in knowing the Lord
10:1-10		False customs of foreigners
	11-16	Living God and false gods
	17-25	Destruction from the north
11:1-17		Punishment for breaking the covenant
	18-23;	Warning to evildoers
	12:1-17	
13:1-11		Parable of the waistcloth
	12-14	Parable of the jars
	15-27	Pride and shame of all
14:1-12		Judeans are beyond deliverance
	13-22	False prophets of peace
15:1-14		Judgment will come
	15-21	Jeremiah pities himself
16:1-13		Threat of exile
	14-21	Promise of return from exile
17:1-10		Cursed man, blessed man
	11-18	God is hope of Israelites
	19-27	Command to keep Sabbath holy
18:1-17		Parable of potter and clay
	18-23	Plot to kill Jeremiah
19:1-15		Parable of the broken flask
20:1-6		Jeremiah defies persecutor Pashhur

	7-18	Jeremiah complains to the Lord
21:1-14		Zedekiah's prayer; God's answer
22:1-9		Oracle about the king's house
	10-17	Oracle about Shallum
	18-30	Oracle about Jehoiakim
23:1-8		Remnant and the true King
	9-15	False prophets to die in shame
	16-22	Call to ignore false prophets
	23-32	False prophets' false dreams
	33-40	Burden of the Lord
24:1-10		Sign of good and bad figs
25:1-14		Judeans' captivity; Babylon's end
	15-29	Cup of the wine of wrath
	30-38	Lord's vengeance
26:1-19		Priests arrest then release Jeremiah
	20-24	Soldiers kill Uriah the prophet
27:1-11		Prophecy of Nebuchadnezzar's victory
	12-22	Promise of exile and return
28:1-17		Jeremiah exposes Hananiah
29:1-23		Letter to the exiles
	24-32	Message to Shemaiah
30:1-17		God will restore His people
	18-24	God will restore Jacob's wealth
31:1-14		God will gather Israelites
	15-22	God will restore Ephraimites
	23-30	God will restore Judeans
	31-40	New covenant
32:1-15		Jeremiah buys a field
	16-25	Jeremiah's prayer
	26-44	Lord's answer
33:1-13		God will restore Israelites
	14-26	Never a lack of king or priests
34:1-11		Zedekiah's broken promise
	12-22	Jeremiah warns of punishment
35:1-11		Rechabites refuse wine
	12-19	Judeans will be punished
36:1-8		Writing on the scroll
	9-19	Reading of the scroll
	20-26	Burning of the scroll
	27-32	Rewriting of the scroll
37:1-10		Chaldeans will return

	11-15	Irijah imprisons Jeremiah
	16-21	King questions Jeremiah
38:1-6		Jeremiah sinks in the mire
	7-16	Ebedmelech rescues Jeremiah
	17-28	Jeremiah's advice to Zedekiah
39:1-18		Babylonians capture Jerusalem
40:1-6		Captain releases Jeremiah
	7-16	Gedaliah's advice to serve Chaldeans
41:1-10		Ishmael murders Gedaliah
	11-18	Johanan routs Ishmael
42:1-22		Jeremiah warns remnant to stay
43:1-7		Flight to Egypt
	8-13	Nebuchadrezzar will destroy Egypt
44:1-10		Lord rebukes the refugees
	11-23	Refugees will perish in Egypt
	24-30	Egypt will be conquered
45:1-5		Encouragement to Baruch
46:1-12		Prophecy about Egypt
	13-24	Prophecy about Nebuchadrezzar
	25-28	Prophecy about Israel
47:1-7		Prophecy against Philistia
48:1-9		Prophecy against Moabites
	10-27	Slackness of the Moabites
	28-36	Pride of the Moabites
	37-47	Shame of the Moabites
49:1-6		Prophecy against the Ammonites
	7-27	Prophecy against the Edomites
	28-33	Prophecy against the Kedarites
	34-39	Prophecy against the Elamites
50:1-16		Prophecy against the Babylonians
	17-34	Israelites will return home
	35-46	Drought and destruction in Babylon
51:1-10		Punishment for the Babylonians
	11-23	Medes execute judgment
	24-33	Babylon a desolation
	34-44	Babylon a heap of ruins
	45-53	People flee
	54-58	Noise of destruction
	59-64	Writings of Jeremiah
52:1-11		Siege and downfall of Jerusalem
	12-23	Destruction of temple

| | 24-30 | Deportation of the Israelites |
| | 31-34 | Honor of Jehoiachin |

LAMENTATIONS **Prophets/Major Prophets**

1:1-7		Jerusalem's desolation
	8-14	Sin of the Israelites
	15-22	Jerusalem is filthy and desolate
2:1-13		Lord's judgment
	14-22	False prophets of Zion
3:1-18		Lament over affliction
	19-39	Hope in God's mercies
	40-54	Plea to return to God
	55-66	Cry for vengeance
4:1-12		Famine in Jerusalem
	13-16	Uselessness of false prophets
	17-22	Peoples' end time
5:1-18		Acknowledgment of disgrace
	19-22	Prayer for mercy

EZEKIEL **Prophets/Major Prophets**

1:1-14		Vision of the four creatures
	15-28	Vision of the four wheels
2:1-7		Commission to go to Israel
	8-10; 3:1-3	Commission to eat the scroll
3:4-11		Commission to speak God's message
	12-15	Visit to Babylon
	16-21	Commission to the watchmen
	22-27	Commission to confinement
4:1-8		Symbol of the siege and exile
	9-17	Symbol of the famine
5:1-4		Symbol of the fall of Jerusalem
	5-17	Desolation of Jerusalem
6:1-7		High places will be destroyed
	8-10	Remnant will be preserved
	11-14	Lord will show He rules
7:1-13		Disaster in the land
	14-27	Desolation of the inhabitants
8:1-6		Vision in the temple
	7-18	Sight of idols and abominations
9:1-11		Slaughter of the idolaters

64

10:1-22		Lord departs from the sanctuary
11:1-12		Ungodly rulers will be punished
	13-25	Hope for the remnant
12:1-16		Unbelief of the people
	17-28	Fulfillment approaches
13:1-16		Prophecy against false prophets
	17-23	Prophecy against false prophetesses
14:1-11		Call to repent
	12-23	Deliverance through righteousness
15:1-8		Parable of the vine
16:1-7		Israelites, an orphan child
	8-14	Israelites, a maiden of beauty
	15-34	Israelites a harlot
	35-43	God judges the Israelites
	44-52	Israel like Sodom and Samaria
	53-63	Promise of restoration
17:1-10		Allegory of the eagles and the cedar
	11-24	Meaning of the allegory
18:1-20		Soul that sins shall die
	21-32	Wicked who repent shall live
19:1-9		Allegory of the lion
	10-14	Allegory of the vine
20:1-13		Israelites' apostasy in Egypt
	14-26	Israelites' apostasy in the wilderness
	27-31	Israelites' apostasy in Canaan
	32-39	God will purge His people
	40-44	God will show mercy to the obedient
	45-49	Prophecy against the Southerners
21:1-7		Lord will draw His sword
	8-17	Condition of the sword
	18-23	Babylonians wield the sword
	24-27	Punishing the prince of Israel
	28-32	Sentence against the Ammonites
22:1-16		Indictment of Israelites
	17-22	Promise of God's wrath
	23-31	Condemnation of Israelites' princes & priests
23:1-10		Sin of the Ohalahites
	11-21	Sin of the Oholibahites
	22-35	Punishing the Oholibahites
	36-49	Judging Oholahites and Oholibahites
24:1-14		Allegory of the boiling pot

	15-27	Ezekiel's wife dies
25:1-11		Prophecies against Ammonites, Moabs
	12-17	Prophecies against Edomites, Philistians
26:1-14		Prophecy against the Tyrians
	15-21	Lament of princes of the sea
27:1-9		Allegory of the ship, Tyre
	10-25	Armies and commerce of Tyre
	26-36	Foretelling the ruin of Tyre
28:1-10		Pride and ruin of Tyrians
	11-19	Lament over king of Tyre
	20-23	Sidon will perish
	24-26	Recovery of Israelite children
29:1-12		Egyptians' pride and desolation
	13-21	Egypt's restoration and plunder
30:1-19		Egypt will perish
	20-26	Promise of Egypt's destruction
31:1-9		Allegory of the cedar of Lebanon
	10-18	Fall of Egypt into the Pit
32:1-16		Lament over Pharaoh
	17-32	Lament over Egypt
33:1-9		Ezekiel, the Israelites' watchman
	10-20	Message of righteousness
	21-29	Jerusalem falls; the land desolate
	30-33	No one heeds the prophet
34:1-10		Prophecy against shepherds
	11-24	Lord God is shepherd
	25-31	Covenant of peace
35:1-15		Prophecy against Mount Seir
36:1-7		Judgment of Israelites' oppressors
	8-15	Israelites will return
	16-21	Punishment for idolatry
	22-32	God will gather Israelites together again
	33-38	Rebuilding of the cities
37:1-14		Vision of dry bones
	15-28	Allegory of the two sticks
38:1-13		Evil scheme of the Gogs
	14-23	Attack and defeat of the Gogs
39:1-16		Burial of the Gogs
	17-24	Sacrificial feast of the Lord
	25-29	God will restore Israelites
40:1-19		Vision of new temple dimensions

	20-37	Location and size of gates
	38-49	Vestibule and its furniture
41:1-26		Nave and walls of the temple
42:1-14		Priests' chambers
	15-20	Size of the temple area
43:1-12		Lord's glory enters the temple
	13-27	Size and use of the altar
44:1-14		Laws about the use of the temple
	15-31	Laws about priests in the temple
45:1-9		Land for priests and prince
	10-25	Laws about weights and offerings
46:1-15		Offerings of the prince
	16-18	Prince and inheritance laws
	19-24	Kitchens for the temple
47:1-12		River flowing from the temple
	13-23	Boundaries of the land
48:1-7		Land for the north
	8-14	Land for priests and Levites
	15-22	Land for city and the prince
	23-29	Land for other tribes
	30-35	Gates of the tribes in Lord's city

DANIEL		**Prophets/Major Prophets**
1:1-7		King chooses four Israelites
	8-21	Test of Daniel and friends
2:1-11		Nebuchadnezzar's forgotten dream
	12-19	Daniel learns the dream
	20-30	Daniel gives thanks to God
	31-45	Daniel interprets the dream
	46-49	King pays homage to Daniel
3:1-7		King sets up an image
	8-15	Plot against the Jews
	16-25	Punishment in the fiery furnace
	26-30	Nebuchadnezzar glorifies God
4:1-18		King tells his dream to Daniel
	19-27	Meaning of dream
	28-33	Punishment of king for pride
	34-37	King repents and recovers
5:1-4		Belshazzar's feast
	5-9	Writing on the wall
	10-16	Belshazzar summons Daniel

	17-30	Daniel announces God's judgment
6:1-9		Men conspire against Daniel
	10-18	Trial of Daniel
	19-24	Daniel in den of lions
	25-28	Darius acknowledges Daniel's God
7:1-8		Daniel's dream of four beasts
	9-14	Everlasting Kingdom
	15-28	Meaning of dream
8:1-14		Vision of the ram, goat and horn
	15-27	Gabriel explains the vision
9:1-19		Daniel's prayer for the people
	20-27	Meaning of the seventy weeks
10:1-21		Daniel's vision of an angel
11:1-4		Four Persian kings shall rise
	5-19	Northerners and Southerners fight
	20-35	Plunder of the land
	36-45	Northern king's power
12:1-4		Time of trouble
	5-13	Command to seal the book

HOSEA		**Prophets/Minor Prophets**
1:1-9		Hosea marries Gomer the harlot
	10-11	Prophecy of restoration
2:1-13		Israelites' adultery and judgment
	14-23	Israelites will be restored
3:1-5		Israelites shall return to the Lord
4:1-13		Israelites' immorality
	14-19	Israelites' adultery
5:1-14		Israelites will be crushed
	15; 6:1-3	Basis for restoration
6:4-6		Sins of Ephraimites and Judeans
	7-10	City of evildoers
	11; 7:1-7	Thieves, bandits, adulterers, intriguers
7:8-10		Aliens in Ephraim
	11-13	Ephraimites are like a silly, senseless dove
	14-16	Turning to Baal
8:1-4		Kings and princes not from God
	5-6	Calf idols
	7-10	Ephraimites and allies

	11-14	Ephraimites' altars for sinning
9:1-6		Egyptians and Assyrians will capture
	7-9	God will punish the peoples' sins
	10-17	God will cast off the Ephraimites
10:1-6		Israelites will be put to shame
	7-10	God will chastise for their double sins
	11-12	Ephraimites will be put to the yoke
	13-15	Tumult of war shall arise
11:1-7		Egyptians will capture the Israelites
	8-12	Israelites will return to their homes
12:1		Ephraimites multiply falsehood and violence
	2-6	God will punish the tribe of Jacob
	7-14	God will punish the Ephraimites
13:1-3		Ephraimites make idols
	4-11	God will devour like a lion
	12-16	Ephraimites and Samarians will die
14:1-9		Wisdom of repentance

JOEL		**Prophets/Minor Prophets**
1:1-10		Plague of locusts
	11-20	Result of the drought
2:1-11		Description of the locusts
	12-17	Call to repentance
	18-27	Lord will restore the land
	28-29	God will pour out His Spirit
	30-32	Signs of the Day of the Lord
3:1-16		Judgment for God's enemies
	17-21	Judah and Jerusalem will be blessed

AMOS		**Prophets/Minor Prophets**
1:1-5		Prophecy against the Damascusians
	6-10	Prophecies against the Gazites and Tyrians
	11-15	Prophecies against the Edomites, Ammonites
2:1-5		Prophecies against Moabites and Judeans
	6-16	Prophecy against Israelites
3:1-8		Israelites' relationship to God
	9-15;	Samarians will be punished
	4:1-3	
4:4-11		Israelites' failure to return to God
	12-13;	Lament for Israel
	5:1-3	

5:4-17		Call to repentance
	18-20	Day of the Lord is darkness
	21-26	Justice, righteousness rather than sacrifice
	27;	Israelites will be exiled
	6:1-14	
7:1-3		Plague of locusts
	4-6	Fire devouring the deep
	7-9	Vision of the plumb line
	10-17	Amaziah tells Amos not to prophesy
8:1-3		Vision of Israel's ruin
	4-6	Lusters of money
	7-14	Events of the Day of Destruction
9:1-10		Sinful people cannot escape punishment
	11-15	God will restore His people

OBADIAH **Prophets/Minor Prophets**

1:1-4		Obadiah sees Edom's fall
	5-9	All of Edom will be destroyed
	10-14	Edomites' sins
	15-16	Judging the peoples
	17-21	Survivors and their possessions

JONAH **Prophets/Minor Prophets**

1:1-10		Jonah flees to a ship
	11-17	Whale swallows Jonah
2:1-9		Jonah's prayer to God
	10	God delivers Jonah from the whale
3:1-9		Jonah preaches in Nineveh
	10	God spares the Ninevites
4:1-5		Jonah asks to die
	6-11	Ninevites worth more than the plant

MICAH **Prophets/Minor Prophets**

1:1-7		God will destroy Samaria and Jerusalem
	8-9	Lament of the prophet
	10-16	Preparation for the destruction
2:1-11		Fate of the wicked and powerful
	12-13	God will gather a remnant together again
3:1-8		Denouncement of Israelites' sin
	9-12	Jerusalem will be destroyed
4:1-5		Coming of law and peace

	6-13	Lord reigns in Zion
5:1-9		Coming Ruler and His reign
	10-15	Idols and weapons will perish
6:1-5		God's complaint against the people
	6-8	What the Lord requires
	9-16	Israelites' corruption
7:1-6		Counsel of despair
	7-14	Trust in God's salvation
	15-20	God's pardon and love

NAHUM — **Prophets/Minor Prophets**
1:1-11		God's vengeance and goodness
	12-15	End of affliction
2:1-9		Siege of Nineveh
	10-13	Cry of desolation
3:1-7		Sins of Ninevites
	8-19	Nineveh will be destroyed

HABAKKUK — **Prophets/Minor Prophets**
1:1-4		People pervert justice
	5-11	Chaldeans will punish the people
	12-17; 2:1	Habakkuk's question about judgment
2:2-5		Life to the righteous
	6-20	Woe to the unrighteous
3:1-15		Glory of the Holy One
	16-19	Rejoicing in the Lord

ZEPHANIAH — **Prophets/Minor Prophets**
1:1-13		All peoples will be judged
	14-18	Day of Wrath
2:1-4		Call to repentance
	5-15	Woe to other peoples
3:1-7		Woe to the Israelites
	8-13	Call to wait for the Lord
	14-20	Call to rejoice

HAGGAI — **Prophets/Minor Prophets**
1:1-11		Call to rebuild the temple
	12-15	People heed the call
2:1-9		Latter house more glorious

	10-14	Holiness and uncleanness
	15-19	God will bless
	20-23	Zerubbabel like a signet ring

ZECHARIAH		**Prophets/Minor Prophets**
1:1-6		Call for all to repent
	7-10	Horsemen who patrol the earth
	11-17	God's cities will prosper again
	18-21	Four horns and four smiths
2:1-13		Holy land will be restored
3:1-10		Joshua receives clean clothes
4:1-14		Lampstand and two olive trees
5:1-4		Flying scroll
	5-11	Ephah of iniquity contains a woman
6:1-8		Four chariots that patrol the earth
	9-11	Order to crown Joshua
	12-15	The Branch will build the temple
7:1-7		Inquiry about fasts
	8-14	Exile is the result of sins
8:1-17		God's intent to restore Jerusalem
	18-23	Peoples to seek God in Jerusalem
9:1-7		Judgment of peoples
	8-10	Triumphant and victorious King
	11-17	King's reign
10:1-12		God to punish the leaders; redeem His people
	11:1-3	
11:4-14		Shepherd doomed to slaughter
	15-17	Woe to the worthless shepherd
12:1-9		Judeans, Jerusalem will prosper
	10-14	Families and land shall mourn
13:1-6		No more false prophets
	7-9	Israelites chastened
14:1-5		Lord will stand on Mount of Olives
	6-11	Reign of the Lord
	12-19	Disobeyers will be punished
	20-21	Pots of sacrifice

MALACHI		**Prophets/Minor Prophets**
1:1-5		Fall of Edomites shows God's love
	6-14	Priests' sins
2:1-9		Warning to the priests

	10-16	Warning to the unfaithful
	17;	Sending the Messiah
	3:1-5	
3:6-12		Call to restore tithes and offerings
	13-15	Stout words against God
	16-18;	Righteous will be spared
	4:1-4	
4:5-6		Elijah will come

MATTHEW		**History**
1:1-17		Genealogy of Jesus
	18-25	Birth of Jesus
2:1-12		Wise men come
	13-18	Joseph, Mary and Jesus flee to Egypt
	19-23	From Egypt to Nazareth
3:1-12		Preaching of John the Baptist
	13-17	John baptizes Jesus
4:1-11		Satan tempts Jesus in the desert
	12-17	Jesus begins His ministry
	18-25	Jesus calls four disciples
5:1-12		Sermon on the Mount
	13-16	Salt and light
	17-20	Righteousness that exceeds
	21-26	Anger and reconciliation
	27-32	Adultery and divorce
	33-42	Oaths and retaliation
	43-48	Neighbors and enemies
6:1-4		Piety and almsgiving
	5-18	Prayer and fasting
	19-24	Possessions and masters
	25-34	Anxieties and God's Kingdom
7:1-6		Judging and hypocrisy
	7-12	Prayer and do unto others
	13-14	Narrow and wide gates
	15-23	Test of false prophets
	24-29	Wise and foolish builders
8:1-4		Jesus heals the leper
	5-13	Jesus heals the centurion's servant
	14-17	Jesus heals Peter's mother-in-law
	18-22	Discipleship
	23-27	Jesus stills a storm
	28-34	Jesus casts out demons
9:1-8		Jesus forgives and heals a paralyzed man
	9-13	Jesus calls Matthew
	14-17	Question about fasting
	18-26	Jesus raises a ruler's daughter
	27-35	Jesus heals blind and dumb men
	36-38	Need for workers
10:1-15		Names and mission of the twelve
	16-25	Facing persecution

	26-33	Value of life
	34-42	Reward of the righteous
11:1-19		Tribute to John the Baptist
	20-24	Judgment of the unrepentant
	25-30	Jesus reveals the Father
12:1-8		Jesus the Lord of the Sabbath
	9-14	Healing on the Sabbath
	15-21	Jesus heals many
	22-37	Jesus answers the Pharisees' slander
	38-42	Warning against seeking signs
	43-45	Return of the unclean spirits
	46-50	Jesus' true family
13:1-9		Parable of the sower
	10-17	Reason for parables
	18-23	Jesus explains the parable of the sower
	24-35	Parables about the Kingdom
	36-43	Jesus explains the parable of the weeds
	44-52	More parables of the Kingdom
	53-58	Nazarenes reject Jesus
14:1-12		John the Baptist dies
	13-21	Jesus feeds five thousand
	22-36	Jesus walks on the sea
15:1-9		Tradition of the elders
	10-20	What defiles a man
	21-28	Canaanite woman's faith
	29-31	Jesus heals multitudes
	32-39	Jesus feeds four thousand
16:1-12		Pharisees ask for a sign
	13-20	Peter says Jesus is the Christ
	21-28	Jesus foretells His resurrection
17:1-13		Transfiguration
	14-21	Jesus heals a boy with epilepsy
	22-23	Jesus foretells His resurrection again
	24-27	Coin in the fish's mouth
18:1-9		Greatest persons in the Kingdom
	10-14	Parable of the lost sheep
	15-22	Sin and forgiveness
	23-35	Parable of the unforgiving servant
19:1-12		Marriage and divorce
	13-15	Jesus blesses the little children
	16-22	Rich young ruler

	57-61	Joseph lays Jesus in the tomb
	62-66	Soldiers seal and guard the tomb
28:1-10		Jesus' resurrection
	11-15	Chief priests bribe the soldiers
	16-20	Great commission

MARK — **History**

1:1-8		Preaching of John the Baptist
	9-13	Baptism and temptation of Jesus
	14-15	Beginning of Jesus' ministry
	16-20	Jesus calls four disciples
	21.28	Jesus casts out unclean spirit
	29-31	Jesus heals Peter's mother-in-law
	32-34	Jesus casts out demons
	35-39	Jesus preaches in Galilee
	40-45	Jesus cleans the leper
2:1-12		Jesus forgives and heals a paralyzed man
	13-17	Jesus calls Matthew
	18-22	Question about fasting
	23-28	Jesus, the Lord of the Sabbath
3:1-6		Jesus heals on the Sabbath
	7-12	Jesus heals many people by the sea
	13-19	Appointing of the twelve
	20-30	Jesus answers the Pharisees' slander
	31-35	Jesus' true family
4:1-9		Parable of the sower
	10-20	Jesus explains the parable of the sower
	21-34	Parables about the kingdom
	35-41	Jesus stills the storm
5:1-20		Jesus casts out demons
	21-43	Jesus raises Jairus' daughter
6:1-6		Nazarenes reject Jesus
	7-13	Mission of the twelve
	14-29	John the Baptist dies
	30-44	Jesus feeds five thousand people
	45-52	Jesus walks on the sea
	53-56	Jesus heals people at Gennesaret
7:1-13		Tradition of the elders
	14-23	What defiles a man
	24-30	Greek woman's faith
	31-37	Jesus heals a deaf and mute man

8:1-10		Jesus feeds four thousand people
	11-21	Pharisees ask for a sign
	22-26	Jesus heals a blind man
	27-30	Peter's statement of faith
	31-38	Jesus foretells His resurrection
9:1-13		Transfiguration
	14-29	Jesus heals the demoniac boy
	30-32	Jesus foretells His resurrection again
	33-50	True disciple
10:1-12		Marriage and divorce
	13-16	Jesus blesses the little children
	17-22	Rich young ruler
	23-31	Kingdom of God
	32-34	Jesus foretells His resurrection
	35-45	Ambition of James and John
	46-52	Bartimaeus receives his sight
11:1-11		Jesus enters Jerusalem
	12-14	Barren fig tree
	15-19	Cleansing of the temple
	20-26	Power of faith
	27-33	Elders challenge Jesus' authority
12:1-12		Parable of the wicked tenants
	13-17	Taxes to Caesar
	18-27	Sadducees and the resurrection
	28-4	Great commandment
	35-7	Question about David's son
	38-0	Jesus' warning against the scribes
	41-4	Widow's offering
13:1-13		Course of this age
	14-23	Time of tribulation
	24-27	Coming of the Son of Man
	28-37	Signs of the end
14:1-2		Plot to kill Jesus
	3-9	Anointing of Jesus at Bethany
	10-11	Bargain of Judas Iscariot
	12-25	Jesus' Passover
	26-31	Jesus foretells Peter's denial
	32-43	Jesus' agony in Gethsemane
	43-52	Soldiers arrest Jesus
	53-65	Jesus before Caiaphas
	66-72	Peter denies Jesus

15:1-15		Jesus before Pontius Pilate
	16-20	Soldiers crown Jesus with thorns
	21-32	Soldiers crucify Jesus
	33-41	Jesus dies
	42-47	Joseph lays Jesus in the tomb
16:1-20		Jesus' resurrection

LUKE		**History**
1:1-4		Preface
	5-13	John the Baptist will be born
	14-25	Song to Zechariah
	26-38	Jesus will be born
	39-46	Mary visits Elizabeth
	47-56	Song of Mary
	57-66	Elizabeth bears John the Baptist
	67-80	Song of Zechariah
2:1-7		Mary bears Jesus in Bethlehem
	8-20	Angels and the shepherds
	21-28	Jesus and his purification
	29-35	Song of Simeon
	36-40	Anna gives thanks to God
	41-52	Boy Jesus in the temple
3:1-20		Preaching of John the Baptist
	21-22	John baptizes Jesus
	23-38	Genealogy of Jesus
4:1-13		Satan tempts Jesus in the wilderness
	14-15	Jesus begins His ministry
	16-30	Nazarenes reject Jesus
	31-37	Jesus casts out unclean spirit
	38-39	Jesus heals Peter's mother-in-law
	40-44	Jesus heals the sick
5:1-11		Jesus calls the first disciples
	12-16	Jesus cleans a leper
	17-26	Jesus forgives and heals paralyzed man
	27-32	Jesus calls Levi
	33-39	Question about fasting
6:1-5		Jesus the Lord of the Sabbath
	6-11	Jesus heals on the Sabbath
	12-16	Jesus chooses the twelve Apostles
	17-19	Jesus heals many
	20-26	Beatitudes and woes

	27-36	Law of love
	37-45	Judging others
	46-49	Wise and foolish builders
7:1-10		Jesus heals a centurion's servant
	11-17	Jesus raises a widow's son
	18-35	Tribute to John the Baptist
	36-50	Anointing of Jesus by sinful woman
8:1-3		Jesus and His followers
	4-8	Parable of the sower
	9-18	Jesus explains the parable of the sower
	19-21	Jesus' true family
	22-25	Jesus stills a storm
	26-39	Jesus casts out demons
	40-56	Jesus raises a ruler's daughter
9:1-6		Mission of the twelve Apostles
	7-9	Herod kills John the Baptist
	10-17	Jesus feeds five thousand people
	18-21	Peter says Jesus is the Christ
	22-27	Jesus foretells His resurrection
	28-36	Transfiguration
	37-43	Jesus casts out an unclean spirit
	44-45	Jesus foretells His resurrection again
	46-50	True disciple
	51-56	Ambition of James and John
	57-62	Discipleship
10:1-16		Mission of the seventy
	17-24	Seventy return
	25-37	Good Samaritan
	38-42	Jesus visits Mary and Martha
11:1-13		Prayer
	14-28	Jesus answers the Pharisees' slander
	29-32	Jesus warns against seeking signs
	33-36	Parable of lighted lamp
	37-53	Warning against Pharisaism
12:1-12		Value of God's people
	13-21	Parable of the rich fool
	22-34	Anxiety
	35-40	Parable of the watching servants
	41-48	Faithful and unfaithful servants
	49-53	Jesus, the Divider
	54-56	Interpreting the present time

	57-59	Settling with an accuser
13:1-5		Jesus calls for repentance
	6-9	Parable of the fig tree
	10-17	Jesus heals a woman on the Sabbath
	18-21	Parables about the kingdom
	22-30	Narrow door
	31-35	Jesus laments over the Jews
14:1-6		Jesus heals on the Sabbath
	7-14	Parable of the marriage feast
	15-24	Parable of the great banquet
	25-33	Parables of the tower and the king
	34-35	Parable of the salt
15:1-7		Parable of the lost sheep
	8-10	Parable of the lost coin
	11-32	Parable of the lost son
16:1-13		Parable of the unrighteous steward
	14-18	Jesus answers the Pharisees
	19-31	Rich man and Lazarus
17:1-10		Faith and forgiveness
	11-19	Jesus heals ten lepers
	20-37	Kingdom in the midst
18:1-8		Parable of the widow and the judge
	9-14	Pharisee and the publican
	15-17	Jesus and the little children
	18-30	Rich young ruler
	31-34	Jesus foretells His resurrection again
	35-43	Jesus heals a blind man
19:1-10		Zacchaeus receives Jesus
	11-27	Parable of the pounds
	28-40	Jesus enters Jerusalem
	41-44	Jesus weeps over the Jews
	45-48	Jesus cleanses the temple
20:1-8		Elders challenge Jesus' authority
	9-18	Parable of the wicked tenants
	19-26	Taxes to Caesar
	27-40	Sadducees and the resurrection
	41-44	Question about David's son
	45-47	Jesus warns against the scribes
21:1-4		Widow's offering
	5-19	Course of this age
	20-24	Jerusalem will be destroyed

	25-38	Signs of the end
22:1-6		Plot to kill Jesus
	7-30	Jesus' Passover
	31-38	Jesus foretells Peter's denial
	39-46	Jesus' agony in Gethsemane
	47-53	Soldiers arrest Jesus
	54-71	Peter denies Jesus
23:1-25		Jesus before Pontius Pilate
	26-31	Jesus on the way to Calvary
	32-38	Soldiers crucify Jesus
	39-43	Penitent thief
	44-49	Jesus dies
	50-56	Joseph lays Jesus in tomb
24:1-12		Jesus' resurrection
	13-35	Jesus walks to Emmaus
	36-43	Jesus appears to the eleven Apostles
	44-49	Great commission
	50-53	Jesus ascends to Heaven

JOHN   **History**

1:1-18		Description of the word
	19-28	John the Baptist's witness to himself
	29-34	John the Baptist's witness to Jesus
	35-42	Andrew and Peter follow Jesus
	43-51	Philip and Nathanael follow Jesus
2:1-12		Jesus turns water into wine
	13-25	Jesus cleanses the temple
3:1-24		Nicodemus visits Jesus
	25-36	John the Baptist's testimony to Jesus
4:1-38		Jesus and the woman of Samaria
	39-45	Conversion of Samaritans
	46-54	Jesus heals the official's son
5:1-18		Jesus heals on the Sabbath
	19-29	Son's witness to the Father
	30-47	Father's witness to the Son
6:1-14		Jesus feeds five thousand
	15-21	Jesus walks on the sea
	22-40	Jesus, the Bread of Life
	41-59	Jews dispute Jesus' claim
	60-65	Some disciples draw back
	66-71	Peter says Jesus is the Christ

7:1-13		Jesus at the Feast of Tabernacles
	14-36	Jesus teaches in the temple
	37-53	Last Great Day of the Feast
8:1-11		Jesus talks to the adulteress
	12-20	Jesus, the Light of the World
	21-30	Jesus warns against unbelief
	31-47	True children of Abraham
	48-59	Jesus is greater than the prophets
9:1-12		Jesus heals the man born blind
	13-34	Pharisees question the healed man
	35-41	Jesus talks to the healed man
10:1-21		Jesus, the Good Shepherd
	22-30	Jesus at the Feast of Dedication
	31-42	Jews try to arrest Jesus
11:1-16		Jesus hears of Lazarus' death
	17-27	Jesus gives eternal life
	28-37	Jesus visits Mary and Martha
	38-44	Jesus raises Lazarus from the dead
	45-57	Plot to kill Jesus
12:1-11		Anointing of Jesus at Bethany
	12-19	Jesus enters Jerusalem
	20-36	Gentiles seek Jesus
	37-43	Many would not believe
	44-50	Summary of Jesus' claims
13:1-20		Jesus washes the disciples' feet
	21-30	Jesus speaks to Judas
	31-35	New commandment
	36-38	Jesus foretells Peter's denial
14:1-11		Way, truth and life from Jesus
	12-14	Some will do greater works
	15-24	Father will send the Holy Spirit
	25-31	Jesus gives His peace
15:1-17		Jesus the True Vine
	18-27; 16:1-4	Hatred from Satan
16:5-15		Jesus will send the Holy Spirit
	16-33	Jesus says He will be gone
17:1-5		Jesus prays to His Father
	6-19	Jesus requests sanctity of disciples
	20-26	Jesus requests sanctity of followers
18:1-11		Soldiers arrest Jesus

	12-27	Jesus before Caiaphas
	28-40	Jesus before Pilate
19:1-16		Soldiers crown Jesus with thorns
	17-27	Soldiers crucify Jesus
	28-37	Jesus dies
	38-42	Joseph lays Jesus in the tomb
20:1-10		Jesus' resurrection
	11-18	Jesus appears to Mary Magdalene
	19-23	Jesus appears to the disciples
	24-31	Thomas doubts, then believes
21:1-14		Jesus appears to the disciples again
	15-25	Jesus questions and commands Peter

ACTS		**History**
1:1-5		Promise of the Holy Spirit
	6-11	Jesus' ascension
	12-26	Matthias replaces Judas
2:1-13		Holy Spirit on Pentecost
	14-36	Peter's talk to the disciples
	37-47	Believers share what they have
3:1-10		Healing of the lame men
	11-26	Peter's talk in the temple area
4:1-4		Elders arrest Peter and John
	5-12	Peter's defense
	13-22	Peter and John go free
	23-31	Report to the disciples
	32-37	Disciples give to the Apostles
5:1-11		God punishes Ananias and Sapphira
	12-16	God adds more believers
	17-32	Elders arrest the Apostles
	33-42	Gamali-el's advice to high priest
6:1-7		Seven men to help widows
	8-15	Elders arrest Stephen
7:1-8		Stephen's defense
	9-16	Age of the patriarchs
	17-34	How Moses led
	35-43	Israelites in the wilderness
	44-53	Worshipping the Most High
	54-60	Men stone Stephen to death
8:1-3		People persecute the Church members
	4-8	Philip at Samaria

	9-25	Simon the sorcerer
	26-40	Ethiopian eunuch converts to God
9:1-9		Saul Paul converts to God
	I0-19	Ananias restores Saul Paul's eyes
	20-22	Saul Paul preaches at Damascus
	23-31	Saul Paul escapes to Jerusalem
	32-35	Peter heals Aeneas
	35-43	Peter raises Tabitha from the dead
10:1-8		Cornelius' vision
	9-16	Peter's vision
	17-23	Cornelius sends for Peter
	24-33	Peter visits Cornelius
	34-43	Peter's talk to Cornelius
	44-48; 11:1-18	Gentiles receive the Holy Spirit
11:19-30		Barnabas and members at Antioch
12:1-5		Herod kills James, arrests Peter
	6-17	Angel frees Peter
	18-25	Herod dies
13:1-12		Saul Paul and Barnabas on Cyprus
	13-43	Paul's preaching in Perga and Antioch
	44-52	Jews oppose; Gentiles believe
14:1-7		Preaching at Iconium
	8-18	Preaching at Lystra
	19-28	Paul and Barnabas return to Antioch
15:1-11		Apostles meet at Jerusalem
	12-21	James' opinion
	22-35	Decision goes to the Gentiles
	36-41	Paul and Barnabas separate
16:1-5		Paul selects Timothy
	6-10	Macedonian call
	11-15	Paul with a family in Lydia
	16-18	Paul casts out divining spirit
	19-24	Owners imprison Paul
	25-40	Philippian jailer converts to God
17:1-9		Paul at Thessalonica
	10-15	Paul at Beroea
	16-33	Paul at Athens
18:1-17		Paul at Corinth
	18-23	Paul returns to Antioch
	24-28	Apollos' preaching at Ephesus

85

19:1-7		Paul baptizes John's disciples
	8-22	Paul's work in Ephesus
	23-41	Demetrius and the riot at Ephesus
20:1-4		Paul visits the Macedonians and Achaians
	5-16	From Philippi to Miletus
	17-38	Paul speaks to the Ephesian elders
21:1-14		Paul travels to Caesarea
	15-26	Paul in Jerusalem
	27-36	Jews arrest Paul
	37-40; 22:1-29	Paul's defense
22:30; 23:1-11		Sanhedrin men try Paul
23:12-22		Plot to kill Paul
	23-35	Soldiers take Paul to Caesarea
24:1-21		Paul before Felix
	22-27	Felix defers the sentence
25:1-12		Paul before Festus
	13-27	Agrippa and Festus discuss Paul
26:1-11		Paul before Agrippa
	12-23	Paul describes his conversion
	24-32	Paul appeals to Agrippa
27:1-12		Journey to Rome
	13-26	Storm at sea
	27-44	Ship crashes
28:1-16		Paul stops over at Malta
	17-31	Paul arrives at Rome

ROMANS		**Epistles of Paul**
1:1-7		Salutation
	8-15	Giving thanks to God through Christ
	16-17	Theme: the Gospel
	18-32	Gentiles: guilty before God
2:1-16		God's principles of judgment
	17-29; 3:1-8	Jews: guilty before God
3:9-20		Everyone: guilty before God
	21-31	Faith: the means of salvation
4:1-25		Abraham's salvation through faith
5:1-11		Results of justification by faith
	12-21	Christ provides basis of salvation

6:1-14		Death and life with Christ
	15-23	Slaves to righteousness
7:1-25		Purpose of the law
8:1-17		Life in the Spirit
	18-30	Glory to come
	31-39	Inseparable from Christ's love
9:1-5		Paul's sorrow for the Israelites
	6-13	Children of the promise
	14-29	Mercy of God
	30-33	Gentiles succeed; Israelites fail
	10:1-13	
10:14-21		Necessity of a preacher
11:1-10		Remnant of Israelites
	11-36	Israelites will receive salvation
12:1-2		Be not conformed to this world
	3-8	How to use gifts
	9-13	How to serve the Lord
	14-21	Overcome evil with good
13:1-7		Obeying government rulers
	8-10	Love your neighbor
	11-14	Put on the armor of light
14:1-12		Do not judge
	13-23	Do not create stumbling blocks
15:1-13		Follow Christ's example
	14-21	Paul's reason for writing
	22-33	Paul's plans to visit
16:1-2		Paul commends Phoebe, a deaconess
	3-16	Roman members to greet
	17-20	Avoid troublemakers
	21-24	Timothy, Tertius, and Gaius say hello
	25-27	Dedication to the Most High God

1 CORINTHIANS		**Epistles of Paul**
1:1-9		Introduction
	10-17	Paul appeals for unity
	18-31; 2:1-5	Christ, the power and wisdom of God
2:6-16		Wisdom of God is a gift of God
3:1-9		Fellow workmen for God
	10-23	Christ, the Foundation
4:1-7		Humility of the Apostles

	8-21	Trials of the Apostles
5:1-8		Report of immorality
	9-13	Judgment of the immoral
6:1-8		Lawsuits among brothers
	9-20	Glorify God in your body
7:1-9		Rights of the married
	10-16	Responsibilities of the married
	17-24	States during calling
	25-38	Counsel to the unmarried
	39-40	Counsel to widows
8:1-13		Food for idols
9:1-12		Apostle's right to receiving material support
	13-18	Paul works for a living
	19-27	All things to all men
10:1-13		Idolaters in the wilderness
	14-22	Do not worship idols
	23-33	Do all to the glory of God
11:1-16		Covering the head
	17-34	Passover bread and wine
12:1-11		Spiritual gifts
	12-26	Unity in diversity
	27-30	Apostles, prophets, teachers
	31;	Way of love
	13:1-13	
14:1-12		Prophecy and tongues
	13-25	Need to interpret tongues
	26-40	Using spiritual gifts
15:1-11		Death of Christ
	12-19	Resurrection of Christ
	20-58	Resurrection of others
16:1-4		Contribution for saints
	5-12	Paul will visit after Pentecost
	13-24	Paul's concluding message

2 CORINTHIANS   **Epistles of Paul**

1:1-14		Affliction
	15-24;	Paul's change of plans
	2:1-4	
2:5-11		Forgiving an offender
	12-17	Paul's triumph in his ministering
3:1-6		Paul's competence from God

	7-18	Splendor in dispensation of righteousness
4:1-6		Paul's honesty in his ministering
	7-18	Paul's trials in his ministering
5:1-10		Paul's courage in his ministering
	11-21	Reconciliation to God
6:1-13		Paul's suffering in his ministering
	14-18; 7:1-4	Temple of God
7:5-16		Rejoicing at good news
8:1-7		Generosity of the Macedonians
	8-15	Jesus' example
	16-24	Titus and messengers are coming
9:1-5		Be ready to give the gift
	6-15	God loves a cheerful giver
10:1-18		Boasting in the Lord
11:1-15		Warning about false preachers
	16-33	Rightful boasting
12:1-10		Visions of the Lord
	11-18	Marks of a true apostle
	19-21; 13:1-4	Paul will not spare the unrepentant
13:5-10		Paul urges examination
	11-14	Paul says farewell

GALATIANS		**Epistles of Paul**
1:1-10		False preachers
	11-24	Paul's authority from God
2:1-10		Acceptance of Paul
	11-21	Paul opposes Cephas
3:1-5		Receiving the Spirit by faith
	6-18	Abraham's example
	19-29	Function of the added laws
4:1-11		Do not return to sin
	12-20	Paul's concern for the Galatians
	21-31	Allegory of Abraham
5:1-12		Legalism threatens liberty
	13-24	Paul defines freedom
	25-26; 6:1-10	Fulfilling the law of Christ

| 6:11-18 | | New creature is what counts |

EPHESIANS — **Epistles of Paul**

1:1-2		Paul's salute
	3-14	Plans for Christ's glory
	15-23	Prayer for wisdom and knowledge
2:1-10		New life with Christ
	11-22	House members of God
3:1-13		Paul, Apostle to the Gentiles
	14-21	Strength through the Spirit
4:1-6		Unity of the Spirit
	7-16	Gifts of the Spirit
	17-32	Old life and new life
5:1-20		Works of light and of darkness
	21-33; 6:1-9	Analogy of family and Church
6:10-20		Whole armor of God
	21-24	Tychicus will tell of Paul

PHILIPPIANS — **Epistles of Paul**

1:1-2		Paul's and Timothy's salute
	3-11	Prayer of thanks
	12-26	Paul's boldness in prison
	27-30; 2:1-11	Christ's example
2:12-18		Obligations of Christians
	19-30	Timothy and Epaphroditus will come
3:1-11		Paul's example
	12-21	Uplifting call of God
4:1-9		Appeal to rejoice in the Lord
	10-20	Acknowledgment of Philippian gifts
	21-23	Hello and goodbye

COLOSSIANS — **Epistles of Paul**

1:1-8		Paul's salute and thanks
	9-14	Paul's prayer for the Colossians
	15-23	Christ, the Expression of God
	24-29; 2:1-7	Paul's ministry
2:8-15		Blotting out of the bond
	16-23	Advice on Sabbath, Festival, and new moon

3:1-17		Christ, the Center of Christian life
	18-25;	Christian family
	4:1-6	
4:7-9		Introducing Tychicus and Onesimus
	10-18	Hello, and final words to follow

1 THESSALONIANS Epistles of Paul

1:1-10		Paul's, Silvanus' and Timothy's salute
2:1-12		Paul's work in Thessalonica
	13-20	Thessalonians' reception of Paul
3:1-10		Timothy's visit and report
	11-13	Prayer for holiness
4:1-8		Appeal for purity
	9-12	Appeal for love and labor
	13-18	Comfort in knowing of the resurrection
5:1-11		Lord will come suddenly
	12-22	Paul appeals for practicality
	23-28	Goodbye

2 THESSALONIANS Epistles of Paul

1:1-2		Paul's, Silvanus' and Timothy's salute
	3-4	Encouragement to endure suffering
	5-12	God judges righteously
2:1-12		Man of lawlessness
	13-17	Thanks and appeal to hold fast
3:1-15		Appeals for prayer and labor
	16-18	Goodbye

1 TIMOTHY   Epistles of Paul

1:1-2		Paul's salute
	3-11	Problem of unsound doctrine
	12-17	Testimony of Paul
	18-20;	Paul urges Timothy to pray
	2:1-8	
2:9-15		Women: dress modestly; not teach; be silent
3:1-7		Required characteristics of a bishop
	8-16	Required characteristics of a deacon
4:1-5		Dealing with false doctrine
	6-10	Instructions for Godly living
	11-16;	Pastor to exemplify the Way
	5:1-2	

5:3-16		Pastoral duties to widows
	17-25	Pastoral duties to elders
6:1-2		Pastoral duties to slaves
	3-10	Warning against false teachers
	11-16	Fighting for the faith
	17-19	Use of wealth
	20-21	Paul's final charge and goodbye

2 TIMOTHY		**Epistles of Paul**
1:1-2		Paul's salute
	3-18	Appeal for faithfulness
2:1-13		Appeal for endurance
	14-26	Workman of God
3:1-9		Apostasy to come
	10-17	Defense of the faith
4:1-8		Charge to preach sound doctrine
	9-22	Hello and goodbye

TITUS		**Epistles of Paul**
1:1-4		Paul's salute
	5-9	Qualifications for elders
	10-16	Dealing with false teachers
2:1-15		Conduct and doctrine of a Christian
3:1-11		Faith and works
	12-15	Final words, and goodbye

PHILEMON		**Epistles of Paul**
1:1-3		Paul's and Timothy's salute
	4-7	Words of thanks to Philemon
	8-22	Appeal for Onesimus
	23-25	Hello and goodbye

HEBREWS		**General Epistles**
1:1-3		Christ, the Revelation of God
	4-14	Christ, the Son of God
2:1-9		Christ's role in salvation
	10-18	Christ, the High Priest
3:1-6		Christ, the Most Glorious
	7-19	Disobedience in the wilderness
4:1-13		Promise of rest
	14-16;	Christ provides the way to the Father

	5:1-10	
5:11-14		Reproving the unskilled in the Word
6:1-8		Warning against apostasy
	9-12	Encouragement of true believers
	13-20	God's oath unchanging
7:1-14		Priority of Melchizedek role
	15-28	Christ's role is superior
8:1-13		New covenant will be superior
9:1-10		Sacrifices only until Christ
	11-14	Sacrifice of Christ
	15-22	Christ: Mediator of coming new covenant
	23-28;	Abolishment of sacrifices
	10:1-18	
10:19-39		Appeal to hold firm
11:1-3		Defining faith
	4-7	Faith of the patriarchs
	8-22	Faith of Abraham and his children
	23-28	Faith of Moses
	29-31	Faith of the Israelites and Rahab
	32-40	Faith of the judges and prophets
12:1-11		Christ's example
	12-29	Appeal for endurance
13:1-6		A few Christian ideas
	7-17	Warning against apostasy
	18-19	Request for prayer
	20-25	Goodbye

JAMES		**General Epistles**
1:1		James' salute
	2-18	Patience in temptation
	19-27	Evidence of belief by conduct
2:1-13		Show no partiality to rich or poor
	14-26	Evidence of faith by works
3:1-12		Evidence of faith by words
	13-18	True and false understanding
4:1-10		Friendship and humility
	11-17	Slander and boasting in arrogance
5:1-6		Miseries of being rich
	7-12	Patience of the saints
	13-20	Pray for one another

1 PETER		**General Epistles**
1:1-2		Peter's salute
	3-9	Salvation by the resurrection of Christ
	10-12	Witness of the prophets
	13-25;	Appeal for a holy life
	2:1-3	
2:4-10		Christ, the Cornerstone
	11-12	Christian and unbelievers
	13-17	Christian and State rules
	18-20	Servant and his master
	21-25	Christ gives the greatest example
3:1-7		Husband and wife
	8-12	Christian's conduct in review
	13-22	Christian and persecution
4:1-11		Christian in the end times
	12-19	Christian and suffering
5:1-14		Christian life in God's care; Goodbye

2 PETER		**General Epistles**
1:1-2		Simeon Peter's salute
	3-11	Growth of true knowledge
	12-21	Basis of true knowledge
2:1-10		False prophets and false teachers
	11-16	Character and conduct of deceivers
	17-22	Consequences of deceiving
3:1-7		Promise of Christ's coming
	8-13	Time and circumstances of His coming
	14-18	Appeal for cleanliness

1 JOHN		**General Epistles**
1:1-4		Introduction
	5-10;	Test of righteousness
	2:1-6	
2:7-17		Test of love
	18-29	Test of belief
3:1-10		Obey God
	11-24	Love one another
4:1-6		Test the spirits
	7-21	Love is of God
5:1-5		Overcome the world by belief

| | 6-12 | Spirit, water, and blood |
| | 13-21 | True God and eternal life |

2 JOHN — **General Epistles**
1:1-3 — John's salute
4-13 — Follow love and follow God; Goodbye

3 JOHN — **General Epistles**
1:1-4 — Rejoicing over gains
5-8 — Support these strangers
9-10 — Diotrephes is doing wrong
11-15 — Imitate the good; Goodbye

JUDE — **General Epistles**
1:1-4 — Contend for the faith
5-16 — Perverters of the truth
17-23 — Stay in the love of God
24-25 — Dedication to the only God

REVELATION — **Apocalypse**
1:1-3 — Revelation of Jesus Christ
4-8 — John's salute
9-20 — Voice and vision
2:1-7 — Message to Ephesus
8-11 — Message to Smyrna
12-17 — Message to Pergamum
18-29 — Message to Thyatira
3:1-6 — Message to Sardis
7-13 — Message to Philadelphia
14-22 — Message to Laodicea
4:1-11 — Father on His throne
5:1-5 — Scroll with seven seals
6-14 — Scroll and the Lamb
6:1-12 — First seal: white horse; rider with bow
3-4 — Second seal: red horse; rider with sword
5-6 — Third seal: black horse; rider and balance
7-8 — Fourth seal: pale horse; rider is death
9-11 — Fifth seal: altar; souls of the saints
12-17 — Sixth seal: earthquake; black sun; red moon
7:1-8 — Sealing of God's 144 thousand servants
9-17 — Saints out of the Tribulation in white robes

8:1-6		<u>Seventh seal</u>: seven trumpets
	7	*First trumpet*: third of earth, trees, grass bur
	8-9	*Second trumpet*: great mountain into the sea
	10-11	*Third trumpet*: Wormwood star from heaven
	12	*Fourth trumpet*: third of sun, moon, stars
	13	Warning of the three woes
9:1-12		*Fifth trumpet*: first woe: locusts
	13-21	*Sixth trumpet*: second woe: Euphrates cavalry
10:1-11		John eats the scroll; seven thunders sound
11:1-14		Two witnesses
	15-19	*Seventh trumpet*: Christ receives Kingdom
12:1-6		Dragon; Mother with child
	7-17	Archangel fights the dragon
13:1-10		Beast from the sea
	11-18	Beast from the earth
14:1-5		Lamb on Mount Zion
	6-20	Angelic messages
15:1-8		Seven bowls of wrath
16:1-2		First bowl: foul and evil sores
	3	Second bowl: sea becomes blood
	4-7	Third bowl: rivers and water become blood
	8-9	Fourth bowl: sun scorches men
	10-11	Fifth bowl: kingdom of the beast in darkness
	12-16	Sixth bowl: kings from the East
	17-21	Seventh bowl: cities fall; plague of hail
17:1-6		Babylon the harlot
	7-18	Explaining the harlot and beast
18:1-8		Angel announces the doom of Babylon
	9-20	Kings and merchants lament Babylon
	21-24	Desolation of Babylon
19:1-10		Marriage supper of the Lamb
	11-21	Christ on His white horse defeats the beast
20:1-3		Angel binds Satan for a thousand years
	4-6	Christ's reign for one thousand years
	7-10	Loosing of Satan
	11-15	White throne; book of life; death & Hades
21:1-8		New heaven and new earth
	9-27	New Jerusalem
22:1-5		Water and tree of life
	6-21	Command about the words of this book